IDEAS AND EVIDENCE

IDEAS AND EVIDENCE

Critical Reflections on
MBTI® Theory and Practice

ROWAN BAYNE

GAINESVILLE, FLORIDA

Published by the Center for Applications of Psychological Type, Inc.
2815 NW 13th, Suite 401
Gainesville FL 32609
352.375.0160 www.capt.org

Center for Applications of Psychological Type, CAPT, and the CAPT logo are trademarks of the Center for Applications of Psychological Type, Inc., in the United States and other countries.

FLEX Care is registered with the United States Patent and Trademark Office.

Myers-Briggs Type Indicator, Myers-Briggs, and MBTI are trademarks or registered trademarks of the Myers-Briggs Type Indicator Trust in the United States and other countries.

Printed in the United States of America

Cover design by Christy Freeman

Library of Congress Cataloging-in-Publication Data

Bayne, Rowan.
Ideas and evidence: critical reflections on MBTI theory and practice /
Rowan Bayne.—1st ed.
     p. cm.
     Includes bibliographical references and indexes.
     ISBN 0-935652-75-2
     1. Myers-Briggs Type Indicator. I. Title.
BF698.8.M94B39 2004
155.2'64–dc22

                                                        2004009473

CONTENTS

FOREWORD

I have known Rowan Bayne for a long time. We meet at various *Myers Briggs Type Indicator® (MBTI®)* events, on my side of the Atlantic or his, and always have intriguing conversations about psychological type. Our dialogues might start with any related topic and they end when we run out of time. You may want to consider this book as a long-distance conversation with Rowan, or better said, as his set of talking points—organized by topics—for the conversation he wants to have with you.

This is a book written for professionals using the MBTI instrument who know (and care) about psychological type—people who are already participants in a probing dialogue about type. It is for readers who want to stretch their understanding of type theory and its effective applications through the challenge of listening to the views of others who may have taken hold of a different part of the elephant.

Rowan is a psychologist and university teacher concerned with personality theory and research and the education of counselors. He brings to this book a broad view of the field of psychology, past and present, with a special concern for the clarity of concepts and language we use in applications of psychological type. His focus is on "the long-standing problem in personality research": "what are the most accurate, useful and central terms, or ways of making sense of experience and behavior?" He prompts us to consider more deeply the common language of our work—the anatomy of the terms such as type and preferences, and our characterizations of the type functions and attitudes. For example, what is the core of the Feeling function? Is it kindness? Or need for harmony? He shares the tracking down he has done of the best descriptors of the traits associated with Extraversion and Introversion, and the other preference pairs.

A glance at the table of contents is almost worthless in some books, but not so with this one. The topics within the chapters are well listed so you can go neatly to the pages you are most interested in. For most of the topics, he presents and comments on the viewpoints and practices of different MBTI practitioners. As you will see, he covers about as many type-related topics as one can imagine: some briefly, some more extensively. He also describes research evidence related to the topics.

Rowan is not shy about giving his opinions on the viewpoints and practices of others, and he frequently offers ideas for new research and for improving the research processes being used. As you can see from the large and rich set of references, he reads widely and stays abreast of the literature on psychological type. Readers interested in the relationships between the MBTI constructs and the Big Five factors in personality research will appreciate Rowan's perspective on this.

Virtually every MBTI practitioner has his or her own favorite exercises for teaching about type. Rowan comments extensively about the relative merits of many of them and describes ones he has devised and the ones he finds most effective.

You may want to argue with Rowan about his viewpoints and emphases, as I do in some instances. No doubt he would like to sit down with you and hear your argument. In reading the book so that I could write this foreword to it, I made notes of a few issues I plan to take up with him next time we have one of our conversations.

Gordon Lawrence
Gainesville, Florida

PREFACE

This book is an evaluation, taking a variety of kinds of evidence into account, of central aspects of *Myers Briggs Type Indicator®* *(MBTI®)* theory and practice. I believe that all kinds of evidence have a part to play, including the expert opinions and observations in the many MBTI books, articles, and websites. However, to improve MBTI theory and practice we need to gather more evidence and more kinds of evidence, and review, integrate, and evaluate it.

I've written the book for MBTI practitioners and researchers—and I hope for those with a more general interest in personality too. The MBTI questionnaire is, after all, the most widely used personality measure for nonclinical populations, and has been for many years. It dominates applied personality theory in the way that Big Five theory dominates personality research.

In chapter 1, I discuss different levels of evidence, the positive skills of critical thinking, and the great variety of research techniques and styles. The prediction from MBTI theory that each of us will probably be more comfortable and skillful with one or two of these techniques than with others may be helpful to individual practitioners and researchers. Chapter 1 is background for the rest of the book, which focuses first on theory and then on applications.

In chapters 2 through 4, the emphasis is on MBTI theory. The main purpose of chapter 2 is to clarify aspects of the two concepts at the heart of the theory: preference and type. In chapter 3 I suggest that, including the preferences, there are eight levels of MBTI theory, and I discuss three of them in particular: temperament, type dynamics, and type development. Chapter 4 is a review of the preferences, probably the most widely used level of the theory. It focuses on what is known and conjectured about core qualities or processes for each preference.

In chapters 5 through 11, the emphasis is on applications, though often with direct implications for theory. Chapter 5 contains a discussion of two central aspects of practice: the aims of MBTI feedback, leading to the issue of evaluating introductory workshops, and ethical problems, particularly bias in language, leading to a general framework for managing such problems.

In chapter 6, I discuss seven issues in verifying MBTI results, especially in designing and running introductory MBTI workshops, and in chapter 7 I review the best exercises to use and the best descriptions of the types. Chapter 8 is a review of several aspects of applying MBTI theory to communication: broad approaches, writing, giving and receiving feedback, and listening. Chapters 9 and 10 contain an examination of what we know about observing type accurately and the most valid clues so far for the preferences and temperaments. In chapter 11 I discuss three diverse applications of MBTI theory to attention deficit hyperactivity disorder (ADHD), job performance, and sport, and I suggest some priorities for MBTI research.

I've assumed a basic knowledge of MBTI theory and practice. There are many good introductions, for example, Myers with Myers (1980) and Martin (1997), and most books on applications include overviews of the theory and descriptions of the preferences and the sixteen types. Some good websites are www.personalitytype.com, which has brief profiles of each type with sections on observing, loving and parenting, communicating with each type, and career choices and each type; www.typetalk.com; www.capt.org ; and guide@mbtypeguide.com.

Finally, I'd like to acknowledge the selective nature of the book. This was necessary because the relevant literature has become so large that to discuss all the interesting and worthwhile issues would result in a catalog. By 2004, the CAPT bibliography had more than 7,800 entries (Johnson 2002), and then there's the wider psychology literature, for example, on personality, especially Big Five theory. However, I also like sifting, reviewing, and choosing; I think of it as beachcombing or—in rarer, possibly J moments—mining. The obvious cost, though, is that there are key issues and pieces of evidence that I've missed or misjudged. I've deliberately omitted most psychometric issues (see Harvey 1996; Myers et al. 1998; and Quenk 2000.)

ACKNOWLEDGMENTS

I am very grateful to the many people with whom I've "talked type" or whose possible types I have observed and thought about. I have particularly enjoyed hundreds of essays and journal entries on type by members of the Postgraduate Diploma in Counselling and Psychotherapy in the School of Psychology at the University of East London. Brief extracts from three journals are included in chapter 5. They are by Helen Lambertini, Alicia Merchant, and Lucy Kaufman.

Then there is *Myers Briggs Type Indicator® (MBTI®)* theory itself. My type—INFP—is said to need an idea, cause, or person to be devoted to, and though I don't much like the term "devoted," it's true for me. MBTI theory, research, and practice have been my main professional interest since 1979. So I would also like to thank very warmly all those who have helped develop MBTI ideas and applications, especially, of course, Isabel Myers and Mary McCaulley, and the many people who helped me with this book, in particular: Gordon Lawrence for his comments on the first draft of the book and for writing a foreword; Leanne Harris for reviewing a later draft; Gillian Hillis and Eleanor K. Sommer for copyediting; Jenny Bimrose (ISTJ) for our many conversations about type; Annette Rogers and Tracy Boakes, who coped with my handwriting and many drafts; and my ISFP wife, Katherine Bayne, who could not (literally could not) answer the MBTI questionnaire, but has added enormously to my understanding and appreciation of MBTI theory and practice.

The list of MBTI vacations in chapter 10 is from OPP's newsletter, *OPPinions*, issue 23, July 2001. It is reproduced with permission from OPP®, the European distributor of the MBTI personality instrument.

Chapter 1

LEVELS OF EVIDENCE

*I*n this chapter I discuss two topics that are background for the rest of the book. The first topic is levels of evidence. The term evidence (and the closely related term research) both apply to a wide range of activities, each with strengths and weaknesses, but essentially both are concerned with finding out how true and useful an idea is. The second topic is critical thinking. I define it in a positive way and discuss several subskills. These skills are also part of gathering and interpreting evidence, and I relate Myers Briggs Type Indicator® (MBTI®) theory to critical thinking and different approaches to research. In the final section I describe and comment on a research study of my own to illustrate some of the earlier points about research and evidence.*

WHAT COUNTS AS GOOD EVIDENCE?

The idea of evidence is central to the approach I take in this book and I try to be both open-minded and skeptical about all levels of evidence. In general terms, evidence means some attempt to support opinions and conjectures with data, argument, or both, and also some attempt to consider alternative interpretations and limitations. For example, the following levels of evidence can underlie a statement like "People with a preference for feeling decision-making (Fs) are gentle," or, more carefully, "Fs tend to be gentle":

LEVEL 1: *Informal observation*—I know 6 people with a preference for F and they're all notably gentle;

LEVEL 2: *Expert opinion*—most writers about type state this;

LEVEL 3: *Empirical evidence*—defining gentleness in terms of a self-report questionnaire and finding that 18 out of 20 Fs scored above average;

LEVEL 4: *Stronger empirical evidence*—as Level 3 but also giving the questionnaire to a sample of people with a preference for T, resulting in data like the following:

TF AND GENTLENESS *(fictitious data)*

		Preference	
		Thinking	Feeling
Gentleness	High	20%	70%
	Low	80%	30%

Although the Level 4 kind of evidence is generally stronger than the other levels, it does not eliminate other kinds and is not decisive. First, there are many questions to ask about it. For example: How valid was the measure of gentleness? How knowledgeable were the participants about MBTI theory, and might their answers have been biased by their knowledge? How did the researcher treat them? Is there just one study giving this result or have other researchers found the same? And so on.

Second, the other levels of evidence, including Level 1, have value too. Informal observations and anecdotes are typically based on large amounts of information, and, if they disagree with more formal sources of evidence, there is a problem to be explained. The explanation may be in terms of biased observation or memory, or stereotyping or a wish to be dramatic, but it may also be that the more formal and apparently more rigorous experiment was poorly designed or flawed and therefore its results are not trustworthy.

More generally, all kinds of evidence have different strengths and weaknesses (Funder 1997; McLeod 1999; Robson 2002). For example, Robson (2002) evaluates survey research as follows:

> Some see the survey as *the* central "real world" strategy. . . . Associated with surveys is a satisfyingly complex set of technological concerns about sampling, question-wording, answer-coding, etc.

> At a practical level, others view surveys as generating large amounts of data often of dubious value. Falsely prestigious

because of their quantitative nature, the findings are seen as a product of largely uninvolved respondents whose answers owe more to some unknown mixture of politeness, boredom and a desire to be seen in a good light than to their true feelings, beliefs or behaviour. (230–31)

Even the "gold standard" method of the double-blind randomized clinical trial (RCT) has its problems (McLeod 2001). In particular, double-blind procedures are difficult to achieve in practice. Moreover, because they are based on group averages they are generally less able to answer questions highly relevant to MBTI theory and practice, such as what kinds of people might benefit most and least from a teaching method or a treatment. However, when an RCT is carried out well, it does have a compelling power (Wessley 2001).

Overall, it is having a variety of methods and researchers, and *how* evidence is gathered and interpreted, that matters most. When it's working well, this cumulative process is informed by critical thinking.

CRITICAL THINKING

The term *critical thinking* may sound positive to some people (perhaps mainly those with a preference for Thinking decision-making or a particular kind of education) but it doesn't to others. Tavris and Wade (1993), for example, defend it as "not merely negative" and then suggest eight guidelines that illustrate to me a predominantly positive meaning. The guidelines, with comments and discussion, are:

1) Ask questions; be willing to wonder.

2) Define the problem.

In practice, defining the problem often means clear and concrete definitions and precise questions. Thus to answer the question, "What makes people happy?" a good definition and measure of *happy* are needed. A problem with guideline 2 (and a difference that may be related to a preference for Thinking versus Feeling) is that there are two opposing views on clear definitions. One is that they're an essential early step, necessary for progress. The other is that some things, especially psychological characteristics, are best defined approximately for the time being at least—that precision is stultifying, can also be premature, and may not be achievable.

3) *Examine the evidence.*

The central issue here is what counts as good evidence. *Examine* implies conducting a reasoned argument and weighing the quality of evidence for and against all the options. Numerous skills and subskills are involved: Ennis (1987) listed 118!

4) *Analyze assumptions and biases.*

5) *Avoid emotional reasoning.*

Here they argue that clear thinking and clear feelings complement each other, that each can be very dangerous used alone.

6) *Don't oversimplify.*

Guideline 6 is about overgeneralizing, as in stereotypes. All the other guidelines for critical thinking can be seen as ways of avoiding oversimplification.

7) *Consider other interpretations.*

8) *Tolerate uncertainty.*

If there is little or no evidence on which to make a judgment, either accept this or be motivated to investigate. This is not to say, "Don't believe in anything"; rather, guideline 8 implies believing with care and being ready to reconsider even the most cherished beliefs.

These guidelines seem to me to respect the strengths of very different MBTI types in their developed forms, but with a leaning toward Intuition (guidelines 1, 7, and 8), Thinking (2, 3, and 4), and Perceiving (8).

KINDS OF RESEARCH

Techniques and styles of research also vary in ways that can be interpreted and organized by MBTI theory. In this section I briefly discuss eight research techniques and four research styles.

Techniques

In psychology generally, there is now a move toward a broader range of methods (Robson 2002; Clifford 2003) and perhaps toward practice-based research as well as research-based practice (Harper, Mulvey, and Robinson 2003). By practice-based research, Harper et al. mean "remaining both accountable for what we do as professionals and able to give a rationale for practice that goes beyond assertion but is based on a wide variety of kinds of evidence" (158). Similarly, Clifford (2003) used the term *evidence-guided practice* (rather than *evidence-based*). He further distinguished between scholarship, which is concerned with "fully understanding what someone else has said and possibly reformulating the account given," and *research*, which is concerned with "the production of new knowledge, new insights, new laws, mechanisms, procedures or processes."

The basic aim of research in psychology is to gather empirical data using one or more of the following techniques (Clifford 2003):

- Quasi-experiments
- Correlational methods
- Interviews
- Questionnaires and surveys
- Observation
- Case studies
- Diary studies
- Archival studies

MBTI practice and research are so far quite heavily biased toward some of these techniques and therefore against others. MBTI practice, for example, is based mainly on qualitative evidence: observation and interviews in which MBTI results are verified against experience.

Styles

Mitroff and Kilman (1978) distinguished between four research styles, each associated with varying combinations of ways to perceive information and make decisions as defined by MBTI theory: "analytical scientists" (associated with preferences for Sensing and Thinking [ST] in their view); "particular humanists" (Sensing and Feeling [SF]); "conceptual humanists'" (Intuition and Feeling [NF]); and "conceptual theorists" (Intuition and Thinking [NT]). Their focus on these combinations of preferences rather than others is supported by research on communication styles (Allen and Brock 2000).

The rationale for Mitroff and Kilman's model is, in part, that scientists tend to

1) measure things precisely and objectively, breaking phenomena down into elements (ST),

2) immerse themselves in the detail of a particular example (SF),

3) study the phenomenon itself from the start (NF), or

4) develop symbolic models and theories in a holistic, skeptical, imaginative, and impersonal way (NT).

MBTI theory thus offers a framework for radically different kinds of evidence and ways of doing research and, further, suggests that they are all valuable and complementary. Some of psychology's methods match well with these styles, for example, controlled experiments with (1) and case studies with (2).

There are numerous good texts on the strengths and weaknesses of different kinds of evidence and research, for example, Robson (2002); McLeod (1999, 2001); and Leong and Austin (1996). There are also lively, sympathetic, and clear discussions of the terrors of statistics (Diamantopoulos and Schlegelmilch 1997) and incisive analyses of such issues as statistical power (Cohen 1988, 1990, 1994); practical versus statistical significance (Haase et al. 1982); and effect sizes (Hedges 1987; Tracey 2000).

Reading the Leong and Austin (1996) *Handbook* is like having a calm conversation with an expert researcher, and it respects and is enthusiastic about the creative, individual nature of all phases of research. Consistent with this, they include a chapter strongly influenced by MBTI theory entitled "Diversity in work styles" (Brenstein 1996).

A SALUTARY EXAMPLE: MY "FULL STOP" STUDY

This study began with the observation, made for no reason that I could tell, that Joan Miro's signature was consistently followed by a full stop (period), and that I liked this; it felt balanced. I started noticing other people's use, or more often nonuse, of a full stop. I checked my own signature in books I'd had for 40 years: my signature had changed in style but was always followed by a full stop.

My next step was to wonder if this was just trivial or whether it might be a clue to type. The most obvious possibility was that the presence of a full stop indicated a preference for J, indicating a desire for closure. However, my type is INFP, so that didn't fit me. The much more exciting possibility was that it indicated the nature—perceptive or judging—of the dominant function. If this subtle possibility was true, then it was of practical value and evidence for type dynamics (which would be very welcome). By this point I was excited and beginning to compose an article for the *Journal of Psychological Type:* "A non-verbal and non-obvious correlate of the dominant function: Evidence for the validity of an aspect of type dynamics."

At the same time as I planned the more formal methodological aspects of the study, I played with the obvious possible meaning of a full stop indicating J (closure, task finished, that's that) or its absence indicating P (open), by not putting a full stop after my signature. It felt odd, not just unfamiliar or new but wrong. Next I asked colleagues whose types I knew to write signatures for me, and their signatures *supported* my hypothesis; thus, another INFP did have a full stop but an ENTP did not and, even better, said that putting one felt unnecessary and obstructive. An INFJ did not have a full stop and neither did an ISTJ. And of course what the ISTJ, INFJ, and ENTP have in common—all they have in common—is a perceiving function as their dominant. It was time for a more rigorous test. I asked about one hundred people whose verified types I knew to report on their current signatures and to seek out examples of their signatures from early in their lives.

The results were very disappointing. First, use of a full stop was too inconsistent to be useful. Second, in those who were consistent, there was no relationship with dominant function. The lesson is that a few observations, however compelling and exciting, are only one kind of evidence. The main problem with a few observations is that they don't show how many exceptions there are or whether something is true in some circumstances and not others. Other kinds of evidence are needed as well.

CONCLUSIONS

To improve MBTI theory and practice, we need to gather more kinds of evidence (and, of course, good quality evidence.) The ideas briefly discussed here, about the different levels of evidence, the positive skills of critical thinking, and the great variety of research techniques and styles, are intended to contribute to making this more likely. One prediction from MBTI theory, that each person will be much more comfortable and proficient in some of these skills, techniques, and styles than others, may also be helpful to individual researchers. In the rest of this book I try to apply the approach to evidence and research outlined in this chapter to key issues in MBTI theory and practice.

Chapter 2

WHAT DO *Preference*
AND *Type* MEAN?

T he first section of this chapter is a general comparison of
Myers Briggs Type Indicator® (MBTI®) theory and the five-
factor theory of personality, also called the Big Five. I draw
on ideas about four of the Big Five factors in this and other
chapters and also on some of this theory's extensive and rigorous
research literature. Then I briefly discuss the relevance of the other
Big Five factor, Neuroticism, to MBTI theory.

In the main section of the chapter, I focus on the two concepts at
the heart of MBTI theory. The first is the meaning of preference. I draw
on the related concepts of "real self," the questions "Is type genetic?"
and "What does 'basic' mean?" and the distinction between constructivist and realist approaches to personality. The second central concept is type. I discuss types and traits, motives, and Reynierse's
critique of MBTI research on type and type dynamics; and place MBTI
theory in relation to other personality theories, drawing in particular
on McAdams's question "What do we know when we know a person?"

MBTI THEORY AND THE BIG FIVE

The five-factor theory of personality has dominated research on personality traits for several years, much as MBTI theory dominates applied
personality theory. Many researchers in the area see it as having substantially resolved the person-situation controversy and the related
problem of the best terms to describe personality. Goldberg (1992), for
example, remarks that "An age-old scientific problem has begun to look

tractable" (26) and McAdams (1992) that "After decades of doubt and defensiveness, traits are back on top" (329). However, the agreement is not unanimous (Eysenck 1992; Block 1995; Matthews and Deary 1998; Funder 2001).

Interpreting and naming the factors is a continuing problem. In personality research generally there are numerous scales with the same name measuring or attempting to measure different characteristics, and other scales with different names that correlate highly. Perhaps the most accepted terms for the Big Five are Extraversion (factor one), Agreeableness (two), Conscientiousness (three), Neuroticism (four), and Openness or Intellect (five).The fifth factor's label is the most problematic.The corresponding MBTI term, Intuition (versus Sensing), may capture its meaning better; it is close to "Imagination," mentioned in passing by Goldberg (1993, 30), and more neutral than Openness or Intellect.

There is a strong relationship at a general level between MBTI theory and Big Five theory (McCrae and Costa 1989; Furnham 1996). For example, McCrae and Costa (1989) gave their self-report and rating measures of the five factors and the then standard form of the MBTI questionnaire to a large sample of the general population. The correlations between the Extraversion and Openness factors of their self-report measure and two of the four MBTI preferences (E–I and S–N) were as high as is likely in this kind of research, and there were substantial correlations between Agreeableness and Conscientiousness and the other two MBTI preferences. Correlations between ratings and MBTI scores were lower but followed the same pattern. These results are very striking: two questionnaires developed in very different traditions (factor analysis and psychotherapy, respectively) agree closely on four of the five most general personality characteristics.

Interpretation of this relationship is more arguable. McCrae and Costa (1989) suggest that although the MBTI descriptions of personality are "reasonably good," it may be better to reinterpret them in terms of the five factor model, to include for example "the antagonistic side of Thinking types and the lazy and disorganized side of Perceiving types" (1989, 36). However, my view is that just as flexibility taken to an extreme becomes disorganization, so extreme Conscientiousness becomes rigidity and obsessiveness rather than organization and self-discipline. The MBTI language, which describes aspects of personality in positive terms first, while adding in effect that strengths have weaknesses, and that strengths can be under- and over-developed, is a much less threatening approach to understanding self and others than the Big Five's—even though it is describing similar behaviors.

Some differences between Big Five and MBTI conceptions at the level of facets, as measured by the MBTI Step II questionnaire, are that in the Big Five approach:

1) Reflection is part of Openness (related to N in MBTI terms) rather than E-I.

2) Warmth is part of E-I rather than Agreeableness (T-F).

3) Openness to Feelings and to Values is part of Openness rather than Agreeableness (T-F).

4) Deliberation—thinking carefully before action—is part of Conscientiousness rather than E-I. (In this respect, Eysenck's "Big Three" model agrees with MBTI theory: impulsiveness is part of E. However, the Eysenck description of E sounds to me most of all like SP.)

Other differences between the two theories are discussed in this chapter and in Bayne (2004).

What about Neuroticism?

Neuroticism, which I will call Anxiety from now on, as a less value-laden and more descriptive term, is the missing characteristic in MBTI theory, or at least from the MBTI questionnaire. Anxiety is firmly established as a major individual difference, yet questionnaire measures of it over-lap substantially with measures of both stress and depression. It is possible to interpret it positively, seeing high Anxiety as sensitive and emotionally rich, low Anxiety as insensitive, bland, and stodgy, but this is stretching its meaning too far. High Anxiety is associated with chronic worrying, moodiness, strain, sleeping badly, and low energy as opposed to calmness and resilience (Matthews and Deary 1998), and for most people it is not reasonable to construe it positively. Therefore it would detract too much from MBTI theory's positive tone to include it in the MBTI questionnaire and in the standard level of interpretation and feedback.

Two points about Anxiety seem worth noting. First, the omission of Anxiety is a clear limitation of the MBTI questionnaire, although there is a good reason for doing so and it does feature (though only on the periphery at the moment) in MBTI theory, as a consequence of type falsification. Second, it has implications for some of the descriptions. For example, the SP temperament is described as "never defeated for long." This is also seen, in mainstream personality theory, as a characteristic of people low on Anxiety. Does this mean that that there is a strong negative correlation between SP and high Anxiety? More generally, are the descriptions of the types, or some of the types, better fits for people who are low on Anxiety?

This is not to equate low Anxiety with good type development, tempting though that may be (cf. K. Myers et al. 1995). Given the genetic basis for Anxiety as a trait, it would mean that people high on Anxiety could not develop and be their psychological type. This seems unlikely because reasonable type development seems to be common. However, the relationship between type, type development, and Anxiety is worth exploring.

THE MEANING OF *Preference*

Preference and type are the two central concepts in MBTI theory, but neither has been discussed in depth or defined formally in the MBTI literature. Preference can be defined simply as "feeling most natural and comfortable with a particular way of behaving and experiencing." For example, someone with a preference for Introversion will, given normal type development and the opportunities, behave introvertedly most of the time and extravertedly some of the time. We can do both, but we prefer one.

Other elements of an adequate definition of *preference* might include "most easily" and "with most interest and energy." Working *best* probably also follows but less directly. Indeed, children who are highly intelligent in the scholastic aptitude sense can be talented in school subjects which do not use their preferences and which therefore, according to MBTI theory, are less fulfilling for them.

"Energy" (and therefore enjoyment/fulfillment) seems to me the central aspect of preference but is not necessarily easy to detect. Another clue for a preference is that while all skills need practice to develop, especially to high levels, MBTI theory suggests that we need less practice with skills related to our preferences, and, conversely, that skills which are related to the opposite preferences to our own usually exist in a relatively pale, undeveloped form. Moreover, even when our "other side" is developed, the theory suggests that it is more tiring to behave in those ways.

Carol Shields provides a vivid illustration of this aspect of preference in relation to Thinking versus Feeling in her novel *The Box Garden*. She does not, however, use these terms, and there is no evidence that she knows about Jung's theory of psychological type or about Myers's clarification and development of it. Her character Charleen muses about the way another character, Eugene, always finds "the most kindly interpretation" of other people's behavior: "Kindness after all comes to him naturally . . . Gentleness, generosity and compromise are not for him learned skills." She contrasts Eugene's natural "kindness" (a central element of the preference for Feeling in MBTI theory) with her own inclinations.

> For me kindness is an alien quality; and like a difficult French verb I must learn it slowly, painfully, and probably imperfectly. . . . It does *not* wake with me in the mornings; every day I have to coax it anew into existence, breathe on it to keep it alive; practice it to keep it in good working order. And most difficult of all, I have to exercise it in such a way that it looks spontaneous and genuine; I have to see that it flows without hesitation as it does from its true practitioners, its lucky heirs who acquire it without laborious seeking, the lucky ones like Eugene. (104)

Here Charleen depicts herself as someone who, despite intense regular practice, has to work very hard to develop and maintain an aspect of her Feeling. In MBTI theory, this means that she is likely to be someone who prefers Thinking. It is unfortunate that she seems not to value her Thinking; gender stereotypes and cultural values are the likely explanations. That she *does* prefer Thinking is supported by two other pieces of evidence: the tone of her musings is analytic and seems naturally so, and in a companion novel, *Small Ceremonies*, Charleen's sister reflects that Charleen "for all her sensitivity, has a core of detachment" (18).

The Charleen example could itself be used in research. Does it trigger parallel examples for the other preferences? A particularly provocative idea in Shields's description is that even after many years of practice (the character Charleen is about thirty-eight years old), it still takes conscious effort every day to keep her kindness—and by extension her Feeling—alive, though she is musing about a very high level of skill. Indeed, she refers to herself as "at the frontier" of these qualities, a vivid metaphor that expresses the oppositeness of the preferences.

Shields's analysis also shows that preference is an underlying and hypothetical concept, in the same way that personality and basic tendencies are. We cannot actually see preferences; we see only the behavior that we interpret. The key practical point here is that the preferences are related to behavior (if we know someone's preference(s), we can explain and predict what they will probably do), but so are lots of other factors, for example, other personality characteristics, mood, the situation, and chance. Behavior is multiply caused.

Preference, therefore, is a summary term for "is more likely to behave in certain ways—which are more fulfilling and more energizing—and less likely to behave in others." The concept of preference thus also makes MBTI theory a fulfillment model of personality; that is, the basic tendencies (a less provocative term than real or true self, but similar in meaning) can be allowed to emerge or can be discouraged. It is what a person does when he or she is "not under the pressure of a time limit or an external reward or coercion. However, situational demands can sometimes blur or mask natural preference" (Quenk 2000, 29).

Another general issue is apparent in Charleen's further reflections. After remarking on Eugene's natural kindness, she also adds that his gentleness is "wound up with the invisible genes which determine the woolliness of his hair and the slightly vacant look in his grey eyes." This issue is explored next from four related perspectives: real self, genetics, the notion of "basic," and realism versus constructivism.

Real Self
The idea of a "real self" in relation to MBTI theory and other personality theories has been discussed at length elsewhere (Bayne 1995). MBTI theory seems to assume that there is a real self in the sense of tendencies and inclinations that are genetically based, but I don't think a genetic basis for type has to be accepted before someone can use the theory. The answer to the question "Where do the preferences come from?" can just be left unanswered or even attributed to early experience. MBTI theory would still be useful.

I find the idea of a genetic real self both appealing and disturbing. It is appealing because it can provide an anchor for our sense of self, and disturbing because, flexible though people are, it sets limits on how much we can change in some core respects (by definition, and barring drugs, brain damage, etc.). Myers put the role of the environment particularly well:

> The finest examples of type development result when children's immediate environment encourages their native capacities. However, when an environment, squarely conflicting with their capacities, forces children to depend on unnatural processes or attitudes, the result is a falsification of type, which robs its victims of their real selves and makes them into inferior, frustrated copies of other people. The greater the original possibilities, the greater the frustration and strain of unfulfillment. (Myers with Myers 1980, 189)

Here she is suggesting that inhibiting one's real self is costly, and that support from parents, guardians, and others is vital, in broad agreement with several major personality theorists, for example, Rogers, Maslow, McCrae and Costa. It might be particularly informative to study people who have changed one preference (like Helen in chapter 3) or even whole types. What is the basis for their decision? What happened earlier in their lives to lead them to create and sustain a false self?

Although I believe that the preferences are inherited, this is not an essential element in the idea of a real self, nor is it straightforward. McCrae and Costa, for example, see some basic tendencies as inherited but others as the result of early experience. Jung would include archetypes in the real self and Freud the "death instinct." And some people (though a small minority in my experience) seem genuinely not to have one or more of the preferences but to be equally comfortable with both sides. It might be useful to know the proportion of people for whom this is true with each preference, and why they have this flexibility (rather than tension) and presumably greater balance. Is the idea of genetic influences consistent with this?

Is Type Genetic?

Here I will briefly discuss research on genetics and personality, drawing first on a discussion of autism by Plomin (2001). In the 1970s autism was thought to be caused by cold, rejecting parents. The parents of autistic children do behave differently toward their children, but the genetic question is, of course, about which comes first. It was investigated through studying identical and nonidentical twins. Autism is rare (about one person in a thousand) but in fifteen children who were diagnosed as autistic and who were identical twins, four pairs of twins were autistic. This is a five-hundredfold increase in risk compared with the general population (and autism is thirty times more likely in children with an autistic sibling than in those with a sibling who is not autistic).

Plomin (2001) discussed various explanations of the finding with twins: genetic, prenatal, the effects of sharing a womb, similarity of experience after birth. He also pointed out that the findings provide strong support for environmental influences on autism too, though not for the idea of cold parenting. Overall his view is that "For self-report questionnaires, most personality traits show moderate genetic influences.... Genes responsible for the heritability of personality are beginning to be identified" (137).

Other researchers suggest that heritability of the Big Five factors—which are clearly related to the preferences, as discussed earlier—is substantial (about 50 percent). For example, Loehlin et al. (1998), using a sample of more than 800 pairs of twins, stated that the Big Five are "substantially and about equally heritable, with little or no contribution of shared family environment" (431). Bouchard and Hur (1998), using the MBTI questionnaire and a smaller sample, found very similar heritabilities. The most dramatic evidence comes from identical twins separated early and growing up in different environments (sometimes very different), yet being much more similar in personality than nonidentical twins and siblings brought up in the same environment. Lykken et al. (1992) give many vivid and detailed examples—far too many, it would seem, to be coincidences.

In addition, the approximate 50 percent figure for heritability of personality does not mean that the other 50 percent is explained by environmental factors (Loehlin et al. 1998). Some of it may be due to interactions among genes, to interactions between genes and environment, to randomness (Miller 1997), to "emergenesis," a concept that Lykken et al. (1992) use to explain genetic traits and talents that don't run in families, and to measurement error (Loehlin et al. 1998).

The phrase "little or no contribution of shared family environment" (Loehlin et al. 1998) is based in part on studies of adopted children brought up in the same family. They were found to be unalike in personality, so their shared environment was not very influential. For many people this finding is extraordinary; their view is that of course some environments produce extraverts, others introverts, and so on.

However, the genetic evidence seems to suggest that this is not the case. McCrae (1994a) calls this evidence "stunning" because of the way it calls into question most personality theories, including those of Rogers and Freud (though I think Rogers's concept of self has a genetic meaning [Bayne 1995]). In contrast, some writers, for example Joseph (2003), see the methodology of the twin and adoption studies as deeply flawed.

My understanding of the complexities of studying genetic and environmental influences is limited, but the following seem to be useful points:

1) The human genome is often compared to a book. Like most metaphors, this is useful but has limitations. The "book" is very large—one person's DNA contains about three billion letters and would take many years to read. Books are linear, but suites of genes switch on and off (usually with perfect timing) and so the book doesn't have an end or a beginning, or even a sequence. The image that comes to mind is of a kaleidoscope or the lights at the end of *Close Encounters of the Third Kind.*

2) A further limitation of the book metaphor is its implication that the genome is a blueprint, when to talk about a gene for, say, Introversion, is much too simple. What is inherited is a predisposition, which is the effect of multiple genes with varying effect sizes. Some outcomes then become more likely, some fairly likely, and some not at all likely, depending on experience (environment).

3) If everyone smoked the same amount, lung cancer would be a genetic disease; if the environment changes, the influence and effects of heredity change, too.

4) As the research on autism illustrates, we are not passive recipients of our environments. Rather, we select, adapt, and create them. For example, musical children seek out music, find it rewarding, seek it out more, and so on. Plomin (2001) suggests the term *appetites* (rather than aptitudes) for this quality. Barnes (2001) expresses the same idea more exuberantly: "Genetic patterns influence which reinforcers we will devote our lives to seeking. Money, diamonds, praise, limelight, approval, love, affection, closeness, ice-cream, gold medals, or the rush—of heroin, of Greek societies, of air moving past our face as we jump from

perfectly good air planes. . . . Reinforcement sounds as if it exists in the outside world but it is the effect on our brain chemistry that makes it a reinforcer" (33).

5) There are also inherited vulnerabilities, a term with a similar flavor to appetites.

Three links between MBTI theory and behavioral genetics seem most useful. The first is that preference and appetites (genetic predispositions) are very similar in meaning, or the same concept. Related analogies are "fertile ground" and "path of least resistance." I see genes as exerting a gentle but constant pressure, though we are also, as a species, very good at learning and adapting.

Second, parents and others can encourage the expression of type, discourage it, or be indifferent to it. MBTI and Big Five theory and research suggest, I think, that most people do develop their types. Therefore, only quite extreme environments can interfere substantially, though different people may also have predispositions of varying degrees of robustness. If we were all brought up in ways that respected and encouraged, or at least did not discourage, our types, those aspects of our behavior related to type would be even more influenced by our genes.

Third, we inherit tendencies or appetites, with a ceiling effect, and the environment, including the womb, shapes their expression. To take a nonpersonality example, one identical twin can get less nutrition than the other in the womb and be shorter at birth as a result, but then catch up if both are given the same, healthy diet when they are babies and children. Rutter and Plomin (1997) discuss this and other subtle aspects of genetics. They argue that high heritability doesn't mean that environmental interventions will be ineffective, that "bad" genes don't justify eugenic programs or terminations of pregnancy, and that some genetic effects increase with age.

What Does *Basic* Mean?

In MBTI theory the four pairs of preferences are the basic characteristics of personality. Other personality theorists have proposed three characteristics (Eysenck), five (McCrae and Costa), and sixteen or more (Cattell), and have also discussed what *basic* means (Eysenck 1992; Costa and McCrae 1992a). Thus, Costa and McCrae (1992a) suggested the following four ways in which their five factors are basic. First, they are real. Self-ratings and ratings by others are highly correlated and stable over several years. Second, they are pervasive. The Big Five factors correlate substantially with most other major personality measures, including the MBTI questionnaire. Third, they are universal. They are found in men and women, in children and adults, and in a wide range of cultures. Fourth, there is evidence of genetic influence, implying differences in brain chemistry. Each of these criteria is also met by the preferences and types in MBTI theory.

Is Personality Real? Constructivist Versus Realist Approaches to Personality

The pure constructivist view of personality is that it doesn't exist but is a perception constructed by the observer. We make it up to help us cope with people's variability. On this view, personality is an example of a general search for and construction of consistency and meaning where there isn't any. More generally, constructivism assumes that there is no objective reality, or if there is, that it is unknowable. An implication is that all theories are equally valuable ways of viewing the world.

The realist view, directly opposed to that of constructivists, is that personality—usually in the form of traits or types—does exist, and that questions about it, and about the related issue of whether or not there are good judges of personality, are sensible and useful. More generally, realism is the belief that scientific theories attempt to describe an objective reality, one that exists separately from ideas about it (Funder 1995, 1999).

Essentialism is a related term. Applied to personality, it assumes an inner essence, which can be discovered, actualized, or denied. It tends to be further assumed by essentialists that personality is inherited or developed very early in life. Constructivists of course reject the idea of an essence, or real self. In research methodology there are related camps: methods which explore the ways in which people make sense of their identities are qualitative (for example, constructing narratives), while methods which test the validity of theories tend to be quantitative. However, the picture here is more complex because some qualitative methods make realist assumptions and others are capable of being used in both constructivist and realist ways.

Realism and constructivism may just be two philosophical positions with no empirical way of deciding between them. However, my view is that the realist position is supported by the evidence on the degree of consistency of people's behavior over time and across situations and the evidence of genetic influences on personality.

THE MEANING OF *Type*

Jung and Myers made the basic assumption (based on observation) that there are different kinds of people, and that the differences are profound ones. Both theories propose that each person's personality is the *opposite* of some others in important respects. They use the term *type* to indicate that people are different in kind and not just in degree: type as a distinctive form, not a convenient language. It attempts to show that people are as different as herons and swans, but with the very significant proviso that while herons behave only like herons, each person can behave like other types of people, indeed, on occasion like all sixteen types. However, and this is the central point in defining preference and type, they do not usually do so with equal facility or with equal fulfillment, and therefore tend to behave like their own type. Given this, the term *type* sounds appropriate (and *style* too superficial).

However, *type* is also a dangerous word for MBTI theory. To some people it suggests a suffocating box or set of boxes. For many psychologists it has connotations of mysticism and charlatanism, and they, too, are put off by what they assume are rigid categories. Against this, and as indicated above, type in MBTI theory has a much more flexible meaning than such fears and rejections allow. It is not used in a pigeonholing way. Each of us can become skillful in behaviors associated with the preferences opposite to our own.

A second danger is apparent here: such flexibility may reflect reality or may be vacuous. A theory of personality that says anyone can behave in any way is extremely weak. Astrology (probably fairly) and psychodynamic theory (perhaps unfairly) have both been attacked on these grounds. MBTI theory is more subtle: it states that most people most of the time behave consistently with their preferences and thus are predictable, but that we can behave in other ways too.

The term *type* is used positively from time to time in the recent literature on personality. For example, Dahlstrom (1995) argued that typologies are an "undervalued and unappreciated" way of thinking about personality organization (8), Vollrath and Torgersen (2002) that "configurations of the basic personality factors, as represented by a typology, may yield clearer results" (1185), which they did, and John and Robins (1994) that "some form of taxonomic system is indispensable" (137). They prefer the term *prototype* because it implies a fuzzy category—one which some people fit more closely than others. For example, sparrows and pigeons are prototypical birds whereas chickens and ostriches are less so, but all four creatures can still be usefully categorized as birds. Another implication of the term prototype is that some people are good examples of more than one type (York and John 1992). MBTI types are prototypes in the fuzzy category sense.

York and John (1992) refer to the distaste for typologies expressed by many personality researchers but see them as "a bridge between purely idiographic and purely nomothetic approaches" (507, cf. Bem 1983), which is highly consistent with MBTI theory and practice. There have been some complex analyses of the psychometric meaning of *type* (e.g., Mendelsohn et al. 1982) but, as in the notion of prototypes, the MBTI types do not have to be discrete to be meaningful (York and John 1992).

MBTI results do not need to be bimodal either. The occasionally successful efforts in MBTI research to find bimodal distributions (Hicks 1984; Rytting et al. 1994), although interesting, are not necessary. I think a simpler meaning of *type* is sufficient for MBTI theory: the structural one in type dynamics, which is essentially a theory of personality organization, with either Sensing (S), Intuition (N), Thinking (T), or Feeling (F) as the dominant function in each type.

Another aspect of structure in MBTI theory is that each preference has a different role and effect in each type. For example, Extraversion in ESFPs is lively, sociable, and present-oriented, while Extraversion in ENTJs is tough-minded and focused on taking actions directed toward future goals. Other differences between type in the MBTI theory sense and trait theories are discussed in the next section.

At a practical research level, four meanings of type can be distinguished in MBTI theory:

- MBTI results or reported type (most of the research uses this definition, and it has the advantage of comparability across studies)
- best fit type (i.e., verification after feedback)
- type in the judgment of expert observers
- true type, in practice usually defined as best fit type, but the

meanings are not identical. MBTI results predict true type, in the best fit sense, about 75 percent of the time on average (Myers et al. 1998, 116).

Types and Traits

MBTI theory has much more to say than trait theory about personality structure. Trait theories neglect the structure and focus on variables rather than on individuals. Trait theories are analogous to describing animals in terms of, say, speed of movement, size, and furriness. For example, an animal can be described as quick, medium size, and quite furry (traits) or as a leopard (type). Thus, the type concept communicates more information more economically than the traits—indeed, *much* more information, especially if the ideas of type dynamics are valid. Researchers into the Big Five and other trait theories of personality could investigate structure but would then be getting close (at least) to developing type theories.

A weaker argument for the superiority of a type approach is that its language is more positive and even-handed. For example, low Conscientiousness in Big Five theory is described as aimless and weak-willed whereas the broad equivalent in MBTI theory is (a) a quality in its own right (Perceiving) and (b) described in terms which are as positive as those describing the broad equivalent of high Conscientiousness (Judging). However, traits don't have to be negative at one end—at least I don't think they do. It's just that they usually are, both in everyday language and in formal trait theories.

Take Openness to Experience, the Big Five broad equivalent of S–N, as an example. In Big Five terms, people high on Openness are, among other qualities, imaginative. The usual interpretation for those low on Openness is that they are unimaginative, but could they be described instead (as they are in MBTI terms) as practical and observant, with a continuum between the two qualities? Is this just a semantic problem, in the same way that *type* sounds as if it refers to discrete categories—this person is an INFP purely and exclusively—when in MBTI theory it has a much more fluid and subtle meaning? Is this criticism of traits an unnecessary inference from the idea that more is good (with exceptions, like Neuroticism) and less is bad?

Indeed, contrary to some accounts, the Big Five language, as used in Costa and McCrae's summary feedback sheet, perhaps because of the influence of MBTI language, is *not* straightforwardly positive at one end of each dimension and negative at the other (Costa and McCrae 1992b, 9). For example, Extraversion is described as "outgoing, active, and high-spirited. You prefer to be around people most of the time" and Introversion as "reserved and serious. You prefer to be alone or with a few close friends." Even low Conscientiousness (the term does not appear on the feedback sheet) is described as "Easygoing, not very well-organized, and sometimes careless. You prefer not to make plans." This is less positive than MBTI descriptions of developed Perceiving—it lacks the MBTI emphasis on such strengths as flexibility and treating work as play—but is not as negative as "aimless" and "weak-willed" (other Big Five descriptions of low Conscientiousness).

In addition, the section later in the NEO-PI Manual on conceptualization and interpretation recognizes negative aspects of the (in its view) positive end of each dimension. For example, "high C is associated with academic and occupational achievement; on the negative side, it may lead to annoying fastidiousness, compulsive neatness, or workaholic behavior" (Costa and McCrae 1992b, 16). The tone is still less even-handed than in the MBTI descriptions but moving in that direction, if a little grudgingly. Therefore, the MBTI descriptions are still much more useful in organizations, couple counseling, and so forth, because they focus on positive qualities and not on deficiencies.

Another difference between trait and type theories is that type theory includes a model of development over the whole life span (Myers, K. and Kirby 1994). This difference has contributed to MBTI theory's success in organizations. However, although Big Five theorists have not yet focused on development, questions about it are compatible with all but an extreme concept of trait (John and Robins 1994).

Motives

The concepts of motive and trait have generally been seen as rivals. Winter et al. (1998) trace their separateness back to the ancient Greeks, through Freud and Jung, then Murray and Allport, to the present day. Both motive and trait have been defined in various ways. Winter et al.'s main argument is that in their most useful senses the two concepts are complementary rather than antagonistic: that "motives involve wishes, desires, or goals (often implicit or nonconscious), whereas traits channel or direct the ways in which motives are expressed in particular actions throughout the life course." In their view, motives are "fundamental goals and desires" (238) and are the main element of the core of personality.

I see Winter et al.'s integrated conception of personality as true of MBTI theory and to a lesser extent of Big Five theory; for example, Extraversion, as used in both these theories, has a motivational element and MBTI theory spells out the main need(s) for each type and temperament. However, unlike some trait theorists, Costa and McCrae (1992b) do discuss and value motives, so the difference in this respect between MBTI theory and Big Five theory, and between both and Winter et al. is only one of emphasis.

A personal example of the practical implications of explanations in terms of motives versus behavior is my usually being early to meetings of all kinds when I have a clear preference for P. My analysis draws mainly on motives:

- I don't want to keep other people waiting (F)
- I'm optimistic about what's going to happen (NF and often unrealistic)
- When I travel somewhere, I allow time for getting lost, sometimes through trying a new route (NP), and often allow more time than I need to.

The same behavior can thus have very different functions for different people, and we need to take both behavior and motives (and experience) into account when trying to understand personality.

Reynierse's Critique of Type

Reynierse (2000) sees the preferences not the types as the core building blocks of MBTI theory. He argued strongly for testing *all* combinations of the preferences: the twenty-four pairs (IJ, etc.), in particular, and the thirty-two triads (IST, etc.), as well as the types. In his view, most of the pairs have been unfairly ignored. His survey (2000) of 131 type tables from articles in the *Journal of Psychological Type* found that each of the twenty-four pairs produced significant effects in about equal amounts. On this evidence, the special status of some pairs such as temperament theory is undeserved. Here, as Reynierse recognizes, he is moving close to the Big Five model and away from type dynamics.

However, it is also a new in-between position, because Reynierse treats the pair effects as interactive (an MBTI theory flavor) rather than additive (Big Five). In his view it also resolves the problem for a type approach of people with unclear preferences. They simply become another variation. This position, which may prove to be the strongest in time, also means the end for type dynamics as a valid theory, so his solution is a drastic one.

At the center of Reynierse's argument is a difficult statistical concept: four-way interactions. The pairs are two-way; types are, in his view, four-way. The problem is partly one of diminishing returns: two-way interactions are powerful enough to explain most relationships, leaving little for triads and types to add. A further difficulty is that four-way interactions, according to a statistics text cited by Reynierse (2000), require "five years of training in a Tibetan monastery simply to comprehend!" (29). If Reynierse's statistical argument is right, MBTI theory at the level of type dynamics and whole types is fundamentally flawed. Moreover, in Reynierse and Harker's (2000) analysis, whole type effects are not apparent using another statistical method (ANOVA) and this—reasonably—strengthens their case for the preferences as the fundamental units. However, there is another approach—to test predictions from type dynamics. If they are supported, and cannot be explained in other ways, such as by Pairs effects, then the four-way interactions argument fails.

A major problem with research on type dynamics—and it may be a significant omission—is that there have been so few studies, and some of these seem unintelligible (or too sophisticated for me). For example, chapter 9 in the latest edition of the *Manual* (Myers et al. 1998) is explicit in its view of "whole type" as "the fundamental unit of analysis" (201), but I find its review of the evidence disappointing, as discussed in chapter 3.

MBTI THEORY AND OTHER PERSONALITY THEORIES

A general issue raised by the motives versus traits question is where MBTI theory belongs in relation to other personality theories. The answer depends on which framework is used. I think it's a Self theory, like those of Rogers and Maslow and, less obviously, the Big Five, but it also transcends the usual categories. A recent, well-received framework from McAdams (1995, 1998) illustrates this. He suggested that individuality can be described at three different levels: (1) traits ("the psychology of the stranger"), (2) "personal concerns" (life tasks, motives), and (3) "integrative life stories" (identity).

Preferences are at level 1. They are broad, stable, and cross-contextual. Motives are at level 2, though McAdams's conception is much broader, including for example life scripts, defense mechanisms, projects, values, and developmental tasks. All these are "characteristic adaptations" in McCrae and Costa's terms. At level 3 we each construct a life story that integrates the past, present, and future to give a sense of identity. Life stories have a plot, heroes and villains, and themes. Examples are "How I was ruined by my family" and "How I triumphed over the past."

"Knowing a person well" therefore means knowing their general tendencies in behavior across situations and over time, knowing how they are adapting and knowing their "stories" about themselves. A list of attributes from levels 1 and 2 is not an identity. McAdams (1995) cautions that level 1 is "well-mapped" but that levels 2 and 3 "need to be explored on their own terms, for a very long time" (386) and that there may be a fourth level.

MBTI theory includes elements of all three of McAdams's levels. Life-themes (Nardi 1999) are a possibility for level 3, as are archetypes, especially if they are used as metaphors, so MBTI theory offers integration, premature or otherwise. Indeed, one of its great strengths is that it explains the variety of other theories. For example, NFPs seem likely to be drawn to Rogers, NTJs and NFJs to Jung, NTs generally to more multilayered, highly abstract theories, and so on. Even if there are lots of exceptions, MBTI theory explains the range of theories, and perhaps the whole range.

Similarly, MBTI theory offers an answer to the question "What is human nature?" It says there are several human natures; each level of the theory suggests a slightly different way of thinking about them. However, let's be sober about this. MBTI theory is a grand theory compared to its rivals, but McAdams is right to be cautious about personality theories and research generally, and there's a lot we don't know yet. But not too cautious! As McCrae (1996) says, in a comparison of McAdams's framework and Big Five theory, the parallels are "a most encouraging sign of the maturing of the field of personality psychology" (353).

CONCLUSIONS

The meaning and value of the concept of preference is a fundamental issue for MBTI theory. People do seem to relate to it easily: we can do both but prefer one. It's also a concept which is echoed in some other theories of personality, notably those of Maslow and Allport, and in the theory which has dominated personality psychology for at least ten years, the Big Five, but I think the concept of preference needs to be clarified and tested further.

The preferences are firmly a part of a realist approach to personality, not constructivist or postmodern. The evidence for genetic influences on closely related personality characteristics provides clear confirmation of their biological reality. Any genetic component at all would do this, but the proportion is a substantial one. It seems to be at least half, but that is with a combination, in MBTI terms, of real self and adapted self so the true proportion may be greater.

Taxonomies play a central role in the natural sciences, but there has been little progress in developing a taxonomy of personality—at least not one that is widely accepted by researchers in the area of psychology in the way that Big Five theory is. Instead of classifying people, Big Five theory classifies variables, which results in a neglect of how personality is organized within each person. *Prototype* and *fuzzy category* are positive and valuable notions, consistent with the MBTI meaning of *type*. Type dynamics is a theory of personality organization, and this is potentially the most useful meaning of type. Trait theories have overshadowed types but McAdams's framework suggests a way of integrating them, and MBTI theory may itself be a good integrating framework for personality.

Chapter 3

HOW USEFUL ARE THE OTHER LEVELS OF MBTI THEORY?

The aims of *Myers Briggs Type Indicator® (MBTI®) theory and practice can in principle be achieved well by using a simple level of the theory: there are people who are sociable and others who are quiet, those who are practical and those who dream, the tough-minded and the gentle, the planners and the spontaneous. The preferences are much subtler, but this simple variation of them, despite the risk of stereotyping, is still useful. However, one of the deep pleasures of MBTI theory is that it has several levels, and in time, much more will be reliably known about which level is most useful for which purposes, and how true each level is. In this chapter, I briefly discuss and evaluate seven levels and some of the relevant research.*

Following are the seven other levels (with the preferences being the first):

- *four temperaments*
- *eight function attitudes*
- *other combinations of the preferences*
- *twenty facets*
- *type dynamics*
- *type development*
- *the "unconscious"*

FOUR TEMPERAMENTS

In his theory of four temperaments, Keirsey (1998; Keirsey and Bates 1978) chose to focus mainly on what people do rather than on hypothetical constructs like dominant function and preference. In this respect, he sees Myers's theory and his own as "rather far apart" (30); Myers et al. (1998) agree with him (59). However, the two theories are often treated as variations of each other, and that is how I see them. Moreover, elements of temperament theory like the core needs and values (Berens 1999) seem to me to be hypothetical constructs.

The four temperaments are defined in MBTI language by four pairs of preferences: SP (which Keirsey [1998] calls Artisan), SJ (Guardian), NT (Rational), and NF (Idealist). A version of the core needs for each temperament, developed from Keirsey, Berens (2000), Delunas (1992), Myers et al. (1998), and others, is described here:

SP	*Excitement, action, freedom*
SJ	*Responsibility, stability, security*
NT	*Analysis, competence, design*
NF	*Support, authenticity, harmony*

The theory assumes that while everyone has a need for excitement, the amount we need and the kind we need varies enormously. For example, SPs need more and more tangible kinds of excitement than the other temperaments do. An important general point here is that such terms are summaries and are most usefully seen in the context of full descriptions. Then it is clear, for example, that for SPs *freedom* means in part: to act on impulse, to respond to the needs of the moment, and to have an impact. Studies of the meanings of key words for people of each temperament could be very illuminating for temperament and MBTI theory, and they work well as exercises (cf. Brock and Allen 2000).

The needs are core in the sense that if they are not met, the result is "psychological death" (Berens 2000). She wrote: "we are energized and truly high functioning only when these core needs are met. To not · have the core needs met is like 'psychological death' and is one source of stress or even dysfunctional behavior" (6). She later refers to people feeling "light of spirit" when their core needs are met, and "drained of energy" when they are not (24). This view is very reminiscent of the conception of "preference" in MBTI theory. Berens also cautions that the core needs can be hard to identify because of life pressures and experiences. This could be a realistic forecast of a methodological difficulty or a way of protecting the theory if research or practice doesn't support it. Either way, I hope the idea of core needs will be rigorously tested soon.

Similar hypotheses can be readily extracted from Keirsey's and Berens's descriptions of the temperaments, and some of these may be easier to test. For example, measurement of mood is now quite established (Thayer 1996), and Berens (2000) states that the "prevailing mood" or "general mood" of each temperament is as follows:

- excitement—SPs (10)
- concern—SJs (12)
- tranquility—NTs (14)
- enthusiasm—NFs (16)

A related issue is the proportion of people described well, though of course only in part, by a single temperament. For example, I think of myself as, very roughly, 80 percent NF, 10 percent SJ, 5 percent NT and 5 percent SP, so NF descriptions tend to fit me well, both as the "major shareholder" and as feeling most essentially me, the most fulfilling aspect. But I also have an SJ flavor or hint of a flavor, and to describe me as, say, "NF with secondary SJ" is more accurate than just "NF" and more manageable than giving percentages.

Similarly, Nardi (1999) suggests that each person rank the four temperaments and that "many people find it easier to first rank one temperament as a *last* choice, then to select one as the temperament they 'could not live without'" (8). However, he too cautions that one's true self—here, true temperament—is "often masked by one's *developed self*" (8). Again, the treacherous word "often" is used, but this position, like that of Berens, detracts from the attractive simplicity of Keirsey's theory. I think it should be tested at a simple level first, then complexities added if necessary.

Keirsey (1998), Berens (1999, 2000), Kroeger and Thuesen (1988), Murray (1995), and others have elaborated on and discussed the nature of the temperaments at length, but empirical research is scarce. Reynierse and Harker (2000) found no greater support for SP, SJ, NT, and NF than for any other pair of preferences. Take, for example, an observation by Kroeger and Thuesen (1988) about the way their guests behave around their pool:

> Our SP guests always grab all the pool toys, head right for the
> water, and invent a new game. The NFs sprawl on the lounge
> chairs and talk earnestly about life and people. The NTs
> dangle their feet in the water, rib each other, and critique the
> issues and people in their professions. And the SJs always,
> always find some work to do, like hanging up towels, husking
> corn, scrubbing the grill, or pulling weeds from the garden. (52)

I find this observation compelling. I feel a shock (a pleasurable one) of recognition. But the empirical questions are how true is it? and how accurate is "always, always"?

Even easier to test would be ideas about the temperaments and choice of clothes and decor, though motives as well as behavior would need to be taken into account. The predictive validity of personality traits is generally modest, though still very useful. Are the temperaments really as powerful as some expert observers state? And how do they compare with the sixteen types and the other levels of MBTI theory for insights and predictive validity?

Another issue for temperament theory and MBTI theory is that they are in direct conflict with each other in some respects. For example, ISFPs and INFPs are very different in temperament theory (SP v NF), but very similar in MBTI theory (both have IF as their dominant function), and the same reasoning applies to several other pairings of types. It seems obvious that we need to clarify which aspects of both theories are the most true and useful.

Of interest too, I think, is the temperament theory perspective on human nature. Often, one basic nature is assumed, for example, Sheldon et al. (2001) asked "What is satisfying about satisfying events?" in an attempt to determine which psychological needs "are truly most fundamental for humans." In contrast, temperament and MBTI theory suggest several human natures, but Sheldon et al.'s methodology could still be used to test the idea of core needs for each temperament.

Overall, empirical research on Keirsey's theory to date seems weak. Myers et al. (1998, 59–63) discuss studies of temperament briefly, but a more detailed review including effect sizes would be useful. Such a review might counter the empirically based criticisms of Reynierse (2000) and the more savage ones of Frisbie (1988), who stated, "Side-stepping conceptual issues, juggling concepts, and adhering to ancient Greek lore seem a questionable way to build a modern personality theory" (14).

EIGHT FUNCTION-ATTITUDES

The function-attitudes are a different level of type theory because they are sometimes used separately from the type dynamics level, and are only one element of it. They were originally proposed by Jung (1923) and have been developed by Thompson (1996a), Berens (1999), and others. The main assumption at this level of MBTI theory is that each preference is significantly different in its extraverted and introverted forms. For example, ES is pleasure loving and laid back and lives in the present, whereas IS is self-disciplined, serious, and traditional. This is quite a contrast!

What ES and IS have in common is, in part, a focus on reality and being practical and observant, and the MBTI questionnaire and results form assume that this characteristic—Sensing—is the major one. Big Five theory makes the same assumption. MBTI theory therefore assumes, at least by implication, that the differences between ES and IS, for example, are not so important, that the characteristics associated with ES and IS are predicted just as well by the preferences for E–I and J–P which follow from them, so the function-attitudes don't add anything. In addition, the differences between the function-attitudes and the preferences are at least partly built into MBTI theory: Extraverts with Sensing dominant are automatically Ps (and of course SPs), and Introverts with Sensing dominant are automatically Js (SJs). The function-attitudes may, therefore, be an unnecessary complication.

The tension here is similar to the one between temperament and MBTI theory and so is the likely resolution. The problems are familiar: broad agreement between different writers but not much empirical evidence. On the positive side, however, there's plenty of scope for interesting and decisive research. For example, in an IS person, does ES tend to be more developed than IN or EN?

OTHER COMBINATIONS

The four pairs of preferences can be combined as sixteen types, thirty-six triads, and twenty-four pairs. Some of the combinations have been discussed much more than others (Reynierse 2000). ST, SF, NT, and NF are probably the most popular pairs, along with the temperaments and function-attitudes, and ES, IS, EN, and IN are regarded as particularly useful in education (Lawrence 1993). It seems likely that some combinations will prove to be the most useful for specific purposes, but I think that testing other aspects of MBTI theory is more important. On the other hand, in most research designs, several levels of MBTI theory can be tested at the same time.

TWENTY FACETS

The twenty facets (five for each pair of preferences) are measured by the MBTI Step II (Kummerow and Quenk 1992; Quenk et al. 2001). Step II could be a misleading term; it is a variation of MBTI theory but not a superior level of it. The MBTI Step I remains the standard measure. The factors in Big Five theory have been divided into facets too, though six rather than five. They are different in name and meaning from the MBTI facets, as briefly discussed in chapter 4. The main issue for the facets is how useful they are compared to the preferences, types, and factors. Research on the Big Five suggests strongly that its facets predict specific behaviors better than the broader factors (Paunonen and Ashton 2001).

The out-of-pattern scores, called "OOPS" by Kummerow and Quenk (1992), though renamed "out-of-preference" scores in Mitchell et al. (1997) and Quenk et al. (2001), are of particular interest for MBTI theory and practice. Someone can, for example, be an Expressive, Imaginative, Questioning ISFJ on their Step II results and verify this with relief and energy. The question arises: are the qualities measured by the three out-of-preference facets in this example true aspects of the person in the same sense as their overall ISFJ preferences are, or are they learned, adaptive aspects? I suspect that true preferences give an overall flavor to a personality while development of one's other side is patchier, more specific to certain situations. For example, an ENFP police officer could be skilled at giving directions but in other respects have relatively or absolutely poor development of Sensing. Depth interviewing seems an obvious methodology to test this idea, perhaps with those types who tend to have detailed recall of the past (SJs) or better analytic abilities (Ts).

In MBTI practice, Step II has proved useful in verifying type, especially the out-of-preference facets. A few MBTI practitioners use only Step II while others use it mainly as a strategy when clients are unclear about their preferences.

TYPE DYNAMICS

The main idea here is that one of the four functions, S, N, T, or F, is dominant, another auxiliary, and so on, and that if people don't use their dominant functions sufficiently, and more than the other functions, they are unlikely to feel fulfilled or at their best. A second intriguing idea is that the *fourth* function, which is the opposite of the dominant, is likely to be the least developed, again with consequences for behavior (Quenk 1993, 1996, 2002). However, I will concentrate here on the dominant function; if it isn't a valid idea, then neither is the rest of type dynamics.

Lawrence (1997) states clearly that the dominant function "plays by far the biggest role in the personality" (11). In other words, given normal development, the dominant function is the most characteristic quality of a person: it "dominates and unifies their life" (Myers with Myers 1980, 10). In terms of motives, K. Myers and Kirby (1994) suggest the following goals for each dominant function (extracted from 12-14):

ES	*to experience as much as possible; to have an unending variety of sensing experience.*
IS	*to form a solid, substantial, and accurate understanding of the world around them and their place in it.*
EN	*to find and explore new possibilities, new and exciting challenges.*
IN	*to develop their inner intuitive patterns for understanding the world.*
ET	*to create logical order in their external world, make their environment rational.*
IT	*to create logical order internally, to develop rational principles for understanding the world.*
EF	*to create harmony and cooperation in their external environment, to facilitate others in getting what they need and want.*
IF	*to develop their internal core of values, establish an external life that is congruent with them, and help both individuals and humankind fulfill their potential.*

(Bayne 1995 suggests variations of these goals as well as metaphors for each dominant function).

I think K. Myers and Kirby also do justice to the intricate and often subtle ideas in MBTI theory. Take, for example, their comment that ISTJs "typically select and store information about what has actually happened within their environment. They often become unofficial historians of their community, their workplace, their family—whatever captures their interest" (6). It is the final phrase that I appreciate most: ISTJs do not file any and all information, as sometimes portrayed.

Nearly all MBTI research to date is on the preferences. The remark "One would be hard-pressed to find more than 10 articles in the last decade that begin with the assumption of the dynamic of the types, which is at the heart of type theory" (Pearman and Fleenor 1996, 28) is still true in 2004, though there have been a few more attempts. I find this puzzling; perhaps Reynierse's view, discussed in chapter 2, explains it. I hope not, but let's review the empirical research that has taken place.

Chapter 9 of the third edition of the *MBTI® Manual* is the obvious starting point. The *Manual*, in contrast to the first two editions, emphasizes type dynamics and whole types throughout, and its chapter 9 reviews the evidence for this central aspect of MBTI theory. Several areas of evidence are discussed (Myers et al. 1998, 196–219), and evaluated as suggesting that "there are characteristics of whole types that are not predictable from knowledge of the individual preferences alone or from simple additive models of the preferences" (219). The chapter conclusion barely mentions its review of evidence on type dynamics— as distinct from whole types—which, considering its importance to type theory, is inadequate in an otherwise generally excellent manual.

The review of research on type dynamics (203–10) starts well by suggesting studies of, for example, dominant Thinking versus auxiliary Thinking (203). Some early studies compared the respective number scores in MBTI results, but this is a basic misuse of those scores (also discussed in Bayne 1995). As the *Manual* states, it is "therefore not a good test of type theory" (204). The next evidence reviewed is from Thorne and Gough's (1991) major work, in which teams of observers in an assessment center rated participants' behavior and gave them a variety of psychological tests. The analysis in the *Manual* of these results seems to me unclear, as does the analysis for the third kind of evidence, based on ANOVA (a standard statistical technique). For evidence to be convincing, it must be presented in a straightforward way. An example of well-presented evidence in the *Manual* is the research on whole types and time orientation by Harrison and Lawrence (1985).

The *Manual* comment on Harrison and Lawrence's results is that they are "particularly impressive" (216). What Harrison and Lawrence found was a nearly perfect correlation of .95 between the sixteen types, in a rank order derived from type dynamics, and how far the types projected themselves into the future. For example, the four dominant intuitive types looked furthest of all. INTJs looked an average of thirty-three years ahead compared with the fifteen years of ENFJs and the eight years of ISFPs.

A colleague and I replicated this study, using a different method (Bayne and Kwiatkowski 1998). The most important reason for the replication of the study was its clear relevance to type dynamics, though we also had doubts about statistical aspects of the interpretation. A rank order correlation of .57 was found, not as remarkable as in the original study but still very high. Considerable variation was also found within each type, one of our concerns at the outset, and one that may reduce the practical significance of the results.

MBTI theory predicts generally clear results: most people of a type are expected to behave most of the time in certain ways and not in others. And the results were not that clear, despite the high correlation. However, I think the design of the study is more likely to be at fault than the theory. (This may be wishful thinking but is readily testable). Specifically, most studies, including these two, examine behavior "in single observations on single occasions" (Epstein 1997, 16)—when several samples of the behavior or characteristic, in this case time orientation, need to be taken and averaged. The MBTI questionnaire does take several samples but of course relies on self-report. It is also better research design not to correlate two self-report measures, especially not two direct and obvious measures.

Overall, the Myers et al. (1998) discussion of research on type dynamics is somewhat obscure and the research surprisingly sparse. Yet the predictions from MBTI theory are clear, and the methodology required for research straightforward. The Mitchell (1991) and Pearman and Fleenor (1996) studies both seem to support type dynamics but use self-report, and self-report and observational data respectively, and more important, are intricately argued, which may make it difficult for people to understand. As Lawrence and Martin (2001) put it, this kind of study does no more than "hint at the reality of type being something beyond simply adding traits from the four preferences" (128). Simpler studies, preferably using performance measures, would be more useful and more engaging.

For example, people with dominant and auxiliary Sensing could be compared on a series of observational tasks. A comparison group of Intuitives would strengthen the study, as would well-established norms for performance on the tasks.

A slightly more refined version of this study, on a different pair of preferences, would be to study the following:

- 10 dominant Ts, 10 auxiliary Ts, 10 dominant Fs, and 10 auxiliary Fs
- One or more valid measures of analytic thinking
- A measure of relative comfort with analytic thinking
- A measure of a quality characteristic of F (perhaps empathy)
- A measure of relative comfort with that characteristic

In addition, the types of the participants should have been verified and attention paid to their motivation. MBTI theory predicts clear differences between the four groups, so forty participants should be enough to confirm the differences, if they exist. (A statistician could advise more precisely on the number of participants needed.)

Is this a good idea? What other relatively straightforward ways are there to test aspects of type dynamics?

TYPE DEVELOPMENT

In normal type development, the dominant function is used most and feels most comfortable. It is an essential part of the person at his or her best. The auxiliary function is used second most. Less often, but ideally, the third and fourth functions are also fairly well developed (K. Myers and Kirby 1994). MBTI theory is optimistic about how developed our preferences tend to be. It assumes that most people's early experience allows or encourages, or at least does not greatly discourage, development of true preferences, a view which is in marked contrast to some major "self" theories of personality, which describe most people as "self-alienated" or "incongruent" (Bayne, 1995).

Thus, taking the optimistic view, a few people will have a preference for Extraversion, for example, but not have developed—used and trusted—it sufficiently to behave in an extraverted manner much of the time. In effect they will be "unfulfilled extraverts": predominantly quiet, private, reserved, and inward, behaving, at least to the casual observer, like genuine introverts. They—and "unfulfilled introverts"—will also, according to the theory, have less sense of self and be less effective.

Ideas about good type development and false type development are discussed by Murphy (1992), Bayne (1995), Quenk (2000), and others. It is easy to picture environmental factors that can impede or suppress type development: a T child who is not allowed to argue, an I who is not allowed time alone, an S who is expected to learn only through words. Two contrasting processes are at work in these examples: (1) discouraging children from using their natural preferences, and (2) encouraging them (probably with love and good intentions) to use the other preferences. Myers with Myers (1980) refers to "falsification of type," a process "which robs its victims of their real selves and makes them into inferior, frustrated copies of other people" (189). Bayne (1995, 2004) discusses an obvious question about type development: "Can it be speeded up?"

A subtle point here is the distinction drawn between developing the *skills* associated with a particular function and *"truly understanding"* that function (K. Myers and Kirby 1994, 32), especially if it's your third or fourth function. K. Myers and Kirby suggest that the quality of the experience is what makes the difference but don't pursue that idea much further, adding only, "It may feel a little surprising and unusual, but it is also refreshing" (32). I believe that using a third or fourth function is not unusual or surprising if you truly understand it, and only refreshing for a while. But the distinction remains a useful one. I also take it to mean that it's more likely (perhaps much more likely) that someone will develop a skill related to a third or fourth function than they will be to develop the whole function. The development of that function will therefore be "patchy."

Various patterns of false type development are logically possible, for example, initially developing the functions in a different order from the one proposed by the theory but later in life recovering to the "right" order. K. Myers and Kirby (1994) suggest "Common development patterns in the first half of life," though I think "problems" is a more accurate term than "patterns," and I wonder how common the following patterns are.

1) Lack of a balancing auxiliary

2) Lack of balance in the attitudes

3) Lack of trust in the dominant function

4) Misuse of the dominant or auxiliary function

Actually, the authors probably do mean patterns because they take quite literally and seriously the ideas that (a) dominant and auxiliary are developed in the first half of life (up to 40 years old or more, optimistically), and (b) third and fourth functions are normally developed most in the second half of life. I would say that both ideas are doubtful, but only on the basis of informal observation. I saw my father, for example, as a mature, emotionally stable, well-developed ISFJ, over seventy years old, but with very little development of N and no signs of its pressing for development. Conversely, I see many people in the first half of life with what seems to me good development of their third and fourth functions. Of course, they may be atypical, and my perceptions may be inaccurate—we don't know. But that's why I would retitle the section "Development problems in the first half of life," but also why it's not a mistake by the authors, as I first thought.

A section of K. Myers and Kirby (1994) that I particularly like is called "Experiencing the function." It includes several exercises for experiencing Sensing and the other functions, again divided into extraverted and introverted variations (34-37) and some wise strategies for guidance, such as "Don't be too ambitious . . ." (33). The exercises are also good practical definitions of the functions.

Another approach to type development is to use guided imagery. Keefer and Yabroff (1995) give a detailed description and Keefer (1995) a case study with someone (an INTP) who wanted to explore her psychological type, in particular to clarify whether she preferred Thinking or Feeling, and to find a way in which the two functions could cooperate.

After six sessions, vividly described and clearly analyzed by Keefer, her client had decided that her first goal did not matter to her and was happy with her new understanding of herself and its effects on her behavior. The imagery had suggested that her Thinking was too dominant—it needed "dethroning"—and her Feeling and Sensing needed to develop, and ways of achieving this. Profound changes seem to have occurred in a short period (the six sessions were about once a week).

It is easy to be skeptical about this level of evidence; the crank literature on medical and psychological therapies is full of miraculous cures. But Keefer's analysis is careful and thoughtful and guided imagery seems worth further study as a counseling technique as well as a method of type development. However, I believe the key issue in this area of MBTI theory and practice is devising a valid measure of type development.

A good measure of type development is unlikely to be a direct self-report measure like the MBTI questionnaire. It will probably be a battery of ability tests, as briefly discussed in Bayne (1995, 68–69). The tests will, I think, need to measure stamina as well as skill (cf. discussion of "preference" in chapter 2). The results will be meaningful both within each person and between people. And it will not be the very successful MTR-i, which measures *use* of the preferences rather than preference itself, or how developed a preference is (S. Myers 2001). A relatively modest but direct and clear start could be made with measuring development of one preference, and using it to test the type dynamics model for the eight types in which it is the dominant or auxiliary.

THE "UNCONSCIOUS"

Spoto (1995) has argued strongly for the power of the unconscious in its dynamic sense. He sees it as "constantly a factor" (121) and is quite scornful of the "tidy and palatable" theory offered by major MBTI writers like Hirsh and Kroeger. In a vivid (but I think inaccurate) metaphor, he sees them as "calmly fishing for minnows from atop the back of a whale" (134). My view is that the dynamic unconscious in the Freudian and Jungian senses is a myth, but a slippery one (Kihlstrom 1999; Spinelli 2001)), and that good evidence for it has not yet been found, despite numerous attempts.

Unconscious is a particularly vague term. Many current psychologists ignore it or see it as wrong or untestable. I think that statements about the unconscious or possible parts of it, like archetypes, that treat it as real rather than a metaphor, are made much too easily. The unconscious in its dynamic sense is not real in the way that a bus or a house is, and the evidence there is for "it" is open to alternative and simpler interpretations. For example, slips of the tongue may reflect conscious feelings or feelings which are just below the surface, rather than hypothetical "deeply submerged" ones, or they may simply be speech errors. When a speaker was congratulated on giving a "millstone" lecture, the host was probably aware of his boredom! Similarly, dreams may be the result of trying to make sense of random brain activity rather than unconscious wishes struggling for expression. They can still be helpful in working out our real emotions, feelings, and intentions but not because they're anything to do with the unconscious.

Contemporary psychology recognizes that we process a lot of information outside awareness but this is a much more gentle conception of unconscious than the dynamic one, more like a robot or a computer than a set of forces or energies (Kihlstrom 1999). Of course Jung thought he went deeper still, into a *collective unconscious*. His evidence was the recurrent myths and images, such as the mandala, in a variety of cultures. An alternative explanation for myths is that they're the result of common human experiences and ways of making sense of them, and that their value is quite separate from an idea like the collective unconscious.

Similarly, *synchronicity* can be explained either as mysterious cosmic forces or by saying: (1) Billions of things are happening at any one moment. (2) Some of them will be very unusual, even incredible, but because so many things happen, so do incredible ones. (3) People tend to see and remember selectively, to search for meaning (and some people also need to believe in mysterious forces). Given these facts, synchronicities become coincidences compounded by the kind of human errors that science tries to counteract. This is not to say that there are no mysteries, that everything can be explained. Rather, it is saying that concepts like collective unconscious and synchronicity can be explained rationally, even though some other things or phenomena cannot (at least not yet).

On the other hand, the unconscious level of MBTI theory does highlight the question of whether or not we *really* know someone's type. It's possible that the relationships between type and behavior are quite often relationships between "false" selves and behavior, with "true" types submerged. This fundamental clash of theories is a recurring one in psychology (see Allport versus Freud, discussed in Bayne [1995]).

A research study bearing directly on this issue of false versus true types would be to take people who had an upbringing supportive of self-expression and who are confident of their type, and measure their types in a relatively objective way, such as with brain-imaging when it becomes more sophisticated, or through DNA, if the links are found. If the same relationships are found in people who did not have such a supportive upbringing (details to be specified), then that would be strong evidence against the validity of the dynamic unconscious level of theory, as spelled out by Spoto and others.

Obviously, we are not in sight of such a study yet, so I rely on the principle of simplicity. In the absence of good evidence *for* the unconscious in its dynamic, thought-to-be profoundly influential sense, and given quite good evidence for the validity of the other levels, and also what seem to me good arguments against the unconscious, I stay with the simpler interpretation: that most people are really the types they seem to be.

There is another current possibility, being energetically pursued by Liz Hallows (1999). I hesitate to include it, despite my claim in chapter 1 to open-mindedness, because of its associations with palmistry, an unproven method for measuring personality. However, I am impressed with her systematic approach. If there are good relationships between preferences, facets, or types and stable characteristics of the hand, then the logic outlined above applies, as it does for any relationships found between genes and MBTI results and brain characteristics and MBTI results.

CONCLUSIONS

The question of which level of MBTI theory is most valid and useful, in general and for particular purposes, is obviously an empirical one. Of the many interesting ideas touched on in this chapter, it seems to me that there are three key areas to be explored through research: tests of aspects of temperament theory, of type dynamics, and of type development. First, I think there are some predictions from temperament theory that could be relatively easily tested, in particular, those about core needs, prevailing moods, and some of the specific behaviors described by Keirsey. If they are supported, it would be positive for the theory, and for justified confidence in applications. If they're not true, or true in limited ways, we really need to know. Second, a measure of the development of some of the preferences (or attitude functions) seems to me within reach. Given a reasonably valid measure of, say, developed Feeling and Thinking, central ideas in type dynamics and type development can be tested and questioned, discarded or refined.

Chapter 4

THE ESSENTIAL AND DEFINING QUALITIES OF EACH PREFERENCE AND TYPE

I*n this chapter, I discuss the essential and defining charac-teristics of each preference and in particular what is its central process or principle, and how good is the evidence so far on this. At the moment, we are only moving toward clarifying these questions.*

Costa and McCrae (1998) discuss six approaches to understand-ing facet-level traits of the Big Five. These can to some extent be applied to the preferences and types. The approaches are (1) rational analysis of item content; (2) characterization of the "low pole, the psychological opposite"; (3) interpretation of external correlates; (4) examination of secondary and tertiary factor loadings; (5) transla-tion into the specialized language of applied psychology; and (6) case studies. Of these, (1) and (4) seem least relevant to the Myers Briggs Type Indicator® (MBTI®) questionnaire, because its items are "straws in the wind"; MBTI theory already does (2); (3) comes under validity and is vitally important; and (5) and (6) have promise for communicating well and deepening understanding rather than as evidence. In particular, they may go some way toward tackling the problem that the Big Five factors, like the preferences, are extremely broad, and their full spectrum of meaning is only poorly captured by the few simple adjectives and phrases generally used to describe them.

In the next four sections, the pairs of preferences are discussed in turn within the following broad structure:

1) The official definition of each preference, from the MBTI Manual (Myers et al. 1998). However, the meaning of each preference is not accurately captured in a few words. There is a risk of being too precise and diminishing them, and it is more a matter of indicating their meaning.

2) *Ideas from the MBTI Step II and the Big Five facets about what might be at the center of each preference. For Quenk et al. (2001, 24) the "core facet" of each preference is the one that correlates most highly with it: Initiating-Receiving with E-I, Concrete-Abstract with S-N, Logical-Empathetic with T-F, and Systematic-Casual with J-P.*

3) *MBTI research.*

4) *Other sources.*

EXTRAVERSION VERSUS INTROVERSION

The *MBTI Manual* definition, following Jung, of *Extraverts* is "those whose energies are primarily oriented outwardly toward people and events in their external environment," and of *Introverts* "those whose energies are directed inwardly toward thoughts and experiences in their inner environment" (Myers et al. 1998, 22).

The basic difference, according to this definition, is where people direct their energy most or most comfortably. The emphasis on thoughts in the definition of Introverts is curious given all the other aspects of inner self-awareness—including emotions, sensations, intuitions, and feelings. However, the most important qualities of both definitions are their breadth and even-handedness.

The five facets for E-I in the MBTI Step II spell out some of the associated ways of behaving, rather than being a formal definition (Kummerow and Quenk (1992, 2003; Quenk et al. 2001). TABLE 4.1 offers a brief summary.

Further, Kummerow and Quenk (1992) suggest that Visual people —the term Visual has now been changed to Reflective—"don't enjoy listening closely to others; when attending a lecture, they often wonder if a paper has been written on the subject that they could just read" (14). This is certainly my experience of lectures (and formal conference papers) but I am also a counselor trainer who particularly enjoys listening closely to others. However, I wouldn't like, or perhaps be able, to listen closely to several clients a day, so again there is the question of how much time in an activity suggests Extraversion, and how much

TABLE 4.1

	(E)	(I)
1)	**Initiating** *More sociable and active*	**Receiving** *More reserved*
2)	**Expressive** *More open about self*	**Contained** *More controlled and private*
3)	**Gregarious** *More friendly and likely to join groups and activities*	**Intimate** *More likely to have a few close friends and not join social groups*
4)	**Active** (previously called Auditory) *Prefers to speak and listen to others*	**Reflective** (previously called Visual) *Prefers to communicate in writing*
5)	**Enthusiastic** *More likely to be lively and the center of attention*	**Quiet** *More likely to be calm and enjoy solitude, seeking the background*

Introversion. Topic may also be a factor; for example, I'm much happier listening to people talking about themselves.

The Big Five definition of Extravert is broader than "sociable" and includes active, assertive, talkative, upbeat, optimistic, and energetic. Introversion is seen as in some respects "the absence of extraversion rather than what might be assumed to be its opposite" (Costa and McCrae 1992b, 15). For example, Introverts are reserved rather than unfriendly and, subtly, "Introverts may say they are shy when they mean that they prefer to be alone: they do not necessarily suffer from social anxiety." The "not necessarily" is somewhat grudging but again there is a flavor of MBTI language and definitely not the more versus less of a characteristic assumed to be part of a trait approach. Indeed, Costa and McCrae state that "Breaking the mental sets that link such pairs as 'happy-unhappy,' 'friendly-hostile,' and 'outgoing-shy' allows important new insights into personality."

When the Big Five and MBTI conceptions of E–I are compared at the level of facets, major differences appear. Those most useful for

MBTI users are possible additions to and refinements of the meanings of the preferences, and the terms used to describe them. Two of the Big Five facets are at least similar to two MBTI facets:

1) Gregariousness—enjoying company and socializing versus not seeking, or even avoiding, company.

2) Assertiveness—dominant and forceful versus keeping in the background.

I think three of the facets expand the MBTI concept a little:

1) Activity—fast-paced, energetic lives versus more leisurely and relaxed, "not necessarily sluggish or lazy."

2) Excitement seeking—bright colors and noise versus quiet.

3) Positive emotions—cheerful and optimistic versus less exuberant and high-spirited, "not necessarily unhappy."

Given this flavor of definition, shy Extraverts and socially skilled Introverts seem particularly worth studying. Extraverts who are shy definitely exist (Cheek and Buss 1981) and seem to be torn between wanting to be sociable and fearful of it, and therefore in a state of tension. They seem worth studying further, partly to explore type development, partly because shyness is reported to be a problem by so many people (about 40 percent [Crozier 2002]). Another large group, socially skilled Introverts, would also be of interest theoretically and in developing applications. Care would be needed though; MBTI theory predicts negative consequences if people are encouraged or trained to disown aspects of their psychological types. On the other hand, type development means supplementing one's main strengths, and assertiveness training appears to work well (Rakos 1991).

The E–I facets also provide vivid illustrations of the long-standing problem in personality research, which is the focus of this chapter. What are the most accurate, useful, and central terms, or ways of making sense of experience and behavior? The best theory will be both simple and subtle in its descriptions, which the OOPS element in MBTI Step II does well, and will capture core underlying qualities.

Lucas et al. (2000) argued that the core quality of E–I is *reward sensitivity,* with sociability a by-product. Part of their argument is that Extraverts are more likely to engage in rewarding situations, and to feel more rewarded in them, than Introverts, and that Extraverts have been found to be happier than Introverts when alone. (Both Extraverts and

Introverts report that social interaction is rewarding, although Extraverts interact more frequently). Lucas et al. (2000) tested this idea about reward sensitivity in thirty-nine cultures varying in how individualist or collective they were. They found a positive relationship between Extraversion and happiness in all cultures, but as predicted, more so in individualistic cultures, because social situations tend to be more rewarding in them.

Ashton et al. (2002) agreed with Lucas et al. that sociability is not the central element of Extraversion, and claimed "the real core is the tendency to behave in ways that attract social attention" (245). They exclude negative or hostile attention and indeed later define the core as "the tendency to engage and enjoy social attention" (250). Therefore, their concept resembles the MBTI Step II facet of Enthusiastic (center of attention) versus Quiet (seeking the background).

On the other hand, if Lucas et al. are right about reward sensitivity, what underlies it? Lucas et al.'s answer is in terms of systems in the brain, as in a related study by Lieberman and Rosenthal (2001) of Introverts and multi-tasking. Lieberman and Rosenthal's research supported the idea that Introverts cope less well with social interaction because there are too many tasks involved and they become overaroused. In terms of brain function, too much catecholamine is produced in the prefrontal cortex. Specifically, Introverts have to choose between nonverbal decoding—observing and interpreting cues from the other person—and talking well. It's not ability but the capacity to multi-task that's the problem.

A practical implication would be for Introverts to interview in pairs or boards rather than alone. Lieberman and Rosenthal also comment that "If life were fair, we might expect introverts to have a nonverbal decoding advantage in non-multi-tasking contexts, but, alas, life is not fair" (307). They do note advantages for Introverts, such as a greater ability to be vigilant, but not many.

Another possible core quality of Extraversion is positive emotions. For some researchers, Extraversion should be renamed Positive Emotionality because the relationship is so strong (Watson and Tellegen 1985; Watson and Clark 1997). For others, the relationship is weaker (Matthews and Deary 1998) and positive emotions are just a part of Extraversion.

More support for the unflattering view of the core of Introversion that seems to be emerging in current personality research comes in

Aron and Aron's work (1997; Aron 1999) with "highly sensitive" people, about 15 percent of the population. Introverts are generally more sensitive to such distractions as temperature and noise than Extraverts, but Aron and Aron were interested in a subgroup. When an advertisement was placed asking for "highly sensitive" people, twenty-four of the thirty-five who completed the MBTI questionnaire were INs, seven ENs, four ISs, and none were ESs. In Aron's (1999) view, the Extraverts were actually Introverts: "Some of the sensitive extraverts grew up in highly social environments; some seemed to have adopted an extraverted persona as a defense and under pressure from family dynamics; others seemed to have adopted an extraverted attitude out of a kind of energetic, restless giftedness" (254). However, some Extraverts may be highly sensitive, just as some are shy.

In a series of studies, Aron and Aron (1997) found that the range of reported sensitivities was extremely wide, for example, to subtleties, caffeine, violence in the media; that high sensitivity was related to but not identical with "social introversion" or with Neuroticism; and that it was associated with intense *positive* emotions (a welcome complexity for Introverts).

One implication of this work is that researchers into Extraversion–Introversion may well find it useful to identify this sensitive group and, Aron (1999) suggests, two subgroups within it. Another is the positive aspect of being highly sensitive as defined by Aron and Aron, especially in a culture that does not appreciate them. For example, this group have a "rich, complex, inner life" (which sounds more like IN), and, when living a "suitable life style," can be *healthier* than others.

The lemon test (Eysenck 1973; Deary et al. 1988) is a particularly interesting example of sensitivity because, like brain imaging, it holds out the hope of a more objective measure of E–I. Four drops of lemon juice are placed on the tongue for twenty seconds, and the amount of saliva produced is compared with the normal amount for that person. Extraverts are less sensitive to the juice and produce much less saliva than Introverts, particularly in the mornings (Deary et al. 1988). The correlation between saliva and E–I is very high (.71 in Eysenck's 1973 study) and has been replicated several times with different methods of collecting saliva, different juice, and so forth (Deary et al. 1988). How would shy Extraverts respond?

The Arons think sensitive people are trying to avoid overarousal.

In their view this group "need to learn a variety of methods to avoid, manage and recover from the stress caused by their greater tendency to become over-aroused. . . . neither overprotecting themselves nor overexposing themselves" (Aron 1999, 266). Aron also suggests a "greater awareness of consequences, both positive and negative" among those who are sensitive, which echoes the idea of "reward sensitivity." More generally, she shares with MBTI theory a respect for diversity of personality.

I wonder whether Introverts are less good at multi-tasking generally, or is the Lieberman and Rosenthal research, assuming that it replicates, about socializing specifically? MBTI theory sees multi-tasking as more associated with the Perceiving preference. Gender is another factor, a major one from Govier's (1998) research. The neuropsychological, brain chemistry aspect of current research is also exciting but full of unknowns at present. Cognitive aspects may be a useful level of intervention. For example, how do people define "reward," and how readily can they redefine it and therefore change their behavior to some extent?

SENSING VERSUS INTUITION

Myers et al. (1998) define *Sensing* as "perceptions observable by way of the senses. Sensing establishes what exists . . . in the present moment" (24). Associated characteristics include being realistic, observant, and practical. *Intuition* is defined as "perception of possibilities, meanings and relationships by way of insight" (24). Associated characteristics include being imaginative, abstract, and oriented toward the future. TABLE 4.2 (page 52) shows the facets of S–N with my summaries.

I think studies of Ss' and Ns' styles of working would be fruitful. Do Intuitive types tend to work in bursts, and if so, all the N types equally? Are all Sensing types systematic? Are the apparently idle periods in between bursts, if they really are characteristic of Ns, more a matter of recovery or of preparation (periods of being fallow rather than arid)? At a more specific level, Woolhouse (1996) examined the differences between Ss and Ns on two ability tests, using a thinking aloud procedure. Intuitive types worked more quickly, using mental short cuts, while Sensing types were more systematic and detailed. Intuitive types were more likely to look for connections, to guess, and to use their intuition, while Sensing types preferred to deal with information that was tangible, detailed, and concrete (Woolhouse and Bayne, 2000).

TABLE 4.2

	SENSING	INTUITION
1)	**Concrete** *More literal, tangible and liking exact facts*	**Abstract** *More drawn to symbolism and original ideas*
2)	**Realistic** *More sensible, matter of fact and efficient*	**Imaginative** *More novel and ingenious*
3)	**Practical** *More pragmatic and results-oriented, like to apply ideas*	**Conceptual** (previously called Inferential) *More interested in knowledge for its own sake*
4)	**Experiential** *More realistic and empirical*	**Theoretical** *More "big picture"— theory and patterns*
5)	**Traditional** *More conventional and valuing of institutions*	**Original** *More unconventional and idiosyncratic*

Two other approaches to understanding the core of S–N are those of McCrae and of Pratt and Gray. First, McCrae (1994b) argued that Openness, the Big Five parallel of N, implies a fluid and permeable structure of consciousness, and that while intellectual *interests* are a "key definer," intellectual *ability* is not. In terms of motives, Openness is an active quest to intensify and enlarge experience, within the fluid structure—Jung himself being a good example (260).

Second, Pratt and Gray (1999) suggested four major differences between S and N at work:

1) Confidence in choices

In their view, Ss need more data, examples, and experience before being comfortable with a decision or theory. This sounds more SJ than SP to me, but ties in with Woolhouse's findings and the Myers with Myers (1980) comment that Sensing types "tend to define intelligence as 'soundness of understanding,' a sure and solid agreement of conclusions with facts" (59). The contrast is with Ns' tendency toward "quickness of understanding" but both abilities are vital in different situations.

2) Time focus
Sensing types tend to be more oriented to the past and present, Intuitive types to the future.

3) Interested in data

4) Scope—comfort with boundaries
The final two differences mean that Ss and Ns seek different data; Pratt and Gray don't specify in what ways, but the obvious characteristics are concrete and tangible (S) versus implicit and nonobvious (N). Their view is that Ss prefer specific and stable boundaries and Ns general and fluid ones, which ties in with McCrae's (1994b) argument about fluidity, and has been further supported by Barbuto and Plummer's (2000) finding that ENFPs tended to report the thinnest boundaries and ISTJs the thickest ones, in Hartmann's sense. But why?

The six Big Five facets of Openness distinguish between different areas of experience. A person is more or less open to Fantasy, Aesthetics, Feelings, Actions, Ideas, and Values. Two remarks by Costa and McCrae about low scorers are the most relevant. Low scorers on Fantasy "prefer to keep their minds on the task at hand," and low scorers on Feelings have "somewhat blunted affects and do not believe that feeling states are of much importance" (Costa and McCrae 1992b). In MBTI terms these apply to Sensing and Thinking respectively. A further useful but minor contribution to understanding S–N here is two of the different areas of experience in which Ns can be imaginative: the arts, and experimenting with new foods and places.

THINKING VERSUS FEELING

Myers et al. (1998) define *Thinking* as a way of making decisions "by linking ideas together through logical connections." It "tends to be objective and impersonal in the application of reason to a decision" (24). Associated characteristics include being analytical and critical, with "an impassive and dispassionate demeanor." *Feeling* "comes to decisions by weighting relative values and merits of the issues."

TABLE 4.3

	THINKING	FEELING
1)	**Logical** *More likely to be impersonal and rely on logic*	**Empathetic** (previously called Affective) *More personal and relying on values*
2)	**Reasonable** *More likely to be impartial and to reason*	**Compassionate** *More likely to be sympathetic*
3)	**Questioning** *More intellectually independent, likes to "zero in on discrepancies"*	**Accommodating** *More likely to approve and be uncritical*
4)	**Critical** *More skeptical, tend to blame more and want proof*	**Accepting** *More tolerant, tend to praise and forgive*
5)	**Tough** *Firmer and more tough-minded*	**Tender** *More gentle, and greater need to be liked and for everyone to look and feel good*

Associated characteristics include warmth and a need for harmony. TABLE 4.3 shows the facets of T-F with my summaries.

I think need for harmony is a central characteristic and motive differentiating between Thinking and Feeling. The related Big Five factor is called "Agreeable," in the sense of pleasant and gentle rather than confirming, which provides some support and a useful term for describing Feeling, despite the comment of Myers with Myers (1980) that "'Agreeable' is too pale a word for the rich personal worth of a feeling evaluation" (65). This point is directed more at the underlying preference than behavior. Low scorers on Agreeableness can be described as ruthless or suspicious, and these descriptions seem to me more likely to be accurate of people with several characteristics: those who have a preference for Thinking and underdeveloped Feeling, and who have been mistreated. (This could, however, be a Feeling bias on my part).

The Big Five facets for Agreeableness are consistent with the MBTI concept of Feeling: Trust, Straightforwardness (in the sense of sincere and ingenuous rather than blunt), Altruism, Compliance, Modesty, and Tender-Mindedness.

Possible gender differences on T–F and their influence are discussed in Bayne (1995) but have not been studied much so far. What proportion of female Ts (especially TJs) present themselves as ultra-feminine—"the art of protective coloration" (Myers with Myers 1980, 66)—for example, and at what cost? MBTI theory and Jung predict tiredness and neurosis respectively for such type falsification.

The terms Thinking and Feeling are particularly open to misuse and bias (along with Judging). They are sometimes misinterpreted as lacking emotions (said of T) and lacking the ability to be logical (said of F). Neither is true, but a subtler version does seem to have some truth. It is that on the one hand Thinking is associated with the view that emotions get in the way of good decisions; they cloud judgment, so they need to be kept in their place. And on the other hand, Feeling is associated with the view, perhaps felt rather than put into words, that logic can miss the point, and that emotions are central in decisions because they tell you what matters most and least to each person involved in or affected by a decision. Disregard emotions at your peril!

That at least is my understanding of the link between T–F and emotions, and it does seem to explain some of the difference. However, it is also said that Ts use *principles* to decide and Fs use *values,* and I wonder if there's a real difference between the two terms, and, if there isn't, whether T decisions may appear more objective and unemotional than they really are. The issue here then is how Ts and Fs treat emotions, and whether the difference lies more in another aspect of T–F: for Fs to be more naturally empathic (and as said earlier, more agreeable) and to focus on the emotions of other people in order to please them more effectively.

Pratt and Gray (2001) proposed six major differences between Thinking and Feeling, which they use to challenge myths and misunderstandings arising from related everyday labels like "hard-boiled" and "soft touch," as well as more technical terms like Thinking and Feeling. In their view, the most useful difference of the six is that "Thinking types seek to improve things. Feeling types seek to build and maintain relationships" (96). The other differences follow from these "primary drives" or motives. Thus, Ts communicate "to get things done," and their language is more about action and results, whereas Fs communicate to "connect with other people," and their language is less crisp and more personal. On the other hand Myers with Myers (1980) suggested that "many of the thinkers' criticisms are not uttered with any expectations of producing change. They are just thrown out in moving from one thought to another" (134). The core quality of Thinking may be more to do with logic and consistency.

In Big Five theory, Agreeable people have "prosocial tendencies" (Graziano and Eisenberg 1997). They tend to behave sympathetically and helpfully. Relevant areas of research include altruism and attachment theory, but I don't think they give any clues to the essential qualities of Thinking and Feeling. Direct support for F and need for harmony comes from Aspendorpf and Wilpers (1998). They studied personality (Big Five) and the social relationships of students for one and a half years, using questionnaires and diaries, and found, translating into MBTI terms, that E–I, T–F, and J–P influenced the number and quality of relationships. In particular, T–F predicted levels of conflict, with Fs having a more peaceful time.

This major study supports (1) the idea that personality influences social and romantic relationships more than the reverse (a fundamental assumption of personality theory) and (2) the idea that the core of F is a need for harmony. But what is the corresponding need in Ts? Why do Ts tend to criticize in a direct way more than they appreciate? Why are they not so interested in being "diplomatic"? One explanation is that for Ts, the risk in conflicts and arguments is that they may be wrong and therefore look incompetent, or (remembering the proposed main motive) not bring about improvement, whereas for Fs the risk is that the relationship will be damaged or end. Needs for achievement and intimacy are related to this stark difference and have a long history in psychology (McAdams 2001).

JUDGING VERSUS PERCEIVING

Myers et al. (1998) define *Judging* as "concerned with making decisions, seeking closure, planning operations, [and] organizing activities" (26), and *Perceiving* as being "attuned to incoming information … open, curious" (27). TABLE 4.4 shows the facets of J–P with my summaries.

As with the other preferences, there are many possible hypotheses to investigate. One of these is multi-tasking, especially clarifying the associated experience and motivation, and its relationship with "Pressure-prompted" (for which "Polyactive" was the first and, I think, better term). Another is longevity, a variable "of obvious importance" (Friedman et al. 1993) and also relatively easy to measure. What Friedman et al. found, very provocatively (especially for Perceiving types), was that people high on Conscientiousness (that is, with a preference for Judging) lived longer, the effect being about as influential as high blood pressure, but less strong than gender or smoking a packet of cigarettes a day if you are a 50-year-old male (181).

TABLE 4.4

	JUDGING	PERCEIVING
1)	**Systematic** *More orderly and more likely to plan thoroughly including for the worst possibilities*	**Casual** *More easygoing and leisurely, and likely to welcome diversions*
2)	**Planful** *More likely to plan long-term and to need to be "settled"*	**Open-ended** *More impulsive and spur of the moment, need not to be "tied down"*
3)	**Early starting** (previously called Stress Avoiding) *As it sounds—the suggested motive is to try to prevent stress*	**Pressure-prompted** (previously called Polyactive) *More last-minute and enjoy the challenge of this*
4)	**Scheduled** *More likely to prefer routine and procedures*	**Spontaneous** *More likely to be uncomfortable with routine and to enjoy the unexpected*
5)	**Methodical** *More likely to make detailed plans for a current task*	**Emergent** *More likely to "wing it," trusting that a solution will emerge.*

However, as with the clear relationship between gender and longevity, the explanation is not straightforward. Friedman et al. suggest that Conscientious people tend to look after their health better, take fewer risks, cooperate with medical treatment more carefully, and cope better with stress. Any or all of these factors, or others, could be vital, and we don't know yet. Moreover, as Friedman et al. point out, the participants in their research grew up in a relatively simple and stable time, and so their finding may not generalize to today's children (and may therefore be more cheerful for Ps!).

Four of the Conscientiousness facets are consistent with the MBTI concept of Judging: Order (neat, tidy, organized); Dutifulness; Achievement Striving; and Self-Discipline. Low self-discipline is distinguished from impulsiveness: "People high in impulsiveness cannot resist doing what they do not want themselves to do; people low in self-discipline cannot force themselves to do what they want themselves to do. The former requires an emotional stability; the latter, a degree of motivation that they do not possess" (Costa and McCrae 1992b, 18).

Another Conscientiousness facet is at odds with J–P. Competence is a "sense that one is capable, sensible, prudent and effective" and, not surprisingly, is associated with high self-esteem. In MBTI theory, competence and self-esteem are not related to J–P and competence is a *major* motive for Ts, and not for Fs. Myers with Myers (1980, 71–73) discusses several elements of Judging and Perceiving, for example, system in doing things (the most logical: TJ, or the most pleasing or proper: FJ) and decisiveness for Js, and spontaneity and adaptability for Ps.

A pure expression of a central part of the preferences for Judging and Perceiving comes in the novel *Spiderweb* (Lively 1998). Nadine and Stella are two young students discussing their different approaches to life.

"The thing about life is to have a strategy," says Nadine. "Ultimate aim, fall-back position." Stella disagrees totally: "The thing about life is to act expediently and creatively. Seize the day. See what comes up and act accordingly." Nadine's approach is consistent with a preference for Judging. Indeed, at the end of the discussion, she proposes a plan of five year checks to see who comes off best: 'I chalk up strategic success and you prove opportunistic gains'" (178–79). In contrast, Stella's statement about being extremely flexible and responding to what comes up is pure Perceiving.

MBTI theory suggests that *both* these strategies are equally likely to work well, but for people who prefer Judging and Perceiving respectively, and that whether Stella or Nadine will "come off best" depends on other factors, like self-confidence, anxiety, and luck, as well as on how much and how purely they act on their probable preferences. The theory's model of development suggests that most Js could usefully add some P to their behavior, and Ps some J, while not losing the strengths of their preference.

CONCLUSIONS

The factors in Big Five theory contribute to understanding the meaning of the preferences, but the central process or principle for each preference is still unclear (as it is for the Big Five). For E–I, the main possibilities so far are arousal (underlying direction of energy and multitasking), reward sensitivity, and positive emotions; for S–N, it's fluidity of boundaries; for T–F, need for harmony and to build and maintain relationships versus to improve things by criticizing them; and for J–P it's a need to be organized versus being flexible.

Chapter 5

THE AIMS AND ETHICS OF MBTI
FEEDBACK AND PRACTICE

yers Briggs Type Indicator® (MBTI®) feedback can be seen as having two general aims: (1) to help people understand and value themselves more, and (2) to understand and value others more. In some circumstances, the aim of understanding others better may take priority over self-understanding. Specific aims follow readily or are sometimes more relevant to a particular group or person than the general aims, which can then remain implicit. Examples of specific aims are to try to improve your chances of getting a job, to identify strengths of yourself and others, to choose a fulfilling career, to build a more effective team, to find the "right" partner, to understand and value your children more, to improve interviewing or interviewee skills, to cope with stress, to solve or manage problems generally, to write more, to influence others, to be a good leader, and so on.

This chapter discusses the two general aims of MBTI feedback. It analyzes some examples of outcomes, suggests more rigorous and systematic methods of evaluation, and reviews some key ethical issues, especially bias in language, and an approach to solving or managing them.

UNDERSTANDING AND VALUING ONESELF

One student on a counseling course reacted to her verified MBTI results as follows: "I felt sort of relieved that I was in one of the 16 squares—as though now I know its OK to be me. I'm official." Another described it as like finding an Owner's Manual to her personality. "Imagine," as Otto Kroeger said to an introductory group in his Basic Three video, "knowing your type ten years ago." Here he's suggesting a refinement of the first aim, one with a J flavor perhaps: that knowing your type enables you to manage yourself better. It puts strengths and weaknesses in a new perspective, suggesting, for example, why each of us finds some activities more tiring than others. Conversely, our type tells us what we're best at and what we really want to do most. According to MBTI theory, the two coincide.

Generally, this level of understanding is confirming and focusing rather than a radical change. The revelation is usually that it's OK after all to be this kind of person, rather than discovering that you're a radically different kind of person. However, as MBTI practitioners know, the latter change happens too. Here is a third counseling student, Helen, writing in her journal (part of the work for the course) at the age of 39 about the effect of a change in one part of her view of herself:

> I now know I am a P.... My view of tasks is becoming more P like and I am actually getting more done.... Understanding I am a P and allowing myself to be a P means I have taken a lot of pressure off myself.... I feel no guilt now about "wasting time." I feel it is not wasted. It is just me allowing myself to do nothing if I choose.

Reading this, talking to Helen about it, and seeing the change in her, was very rewarding for me too. Discovering your psychological type can be extremely liberating and affirming. Things fall into place. Puzzling aspects of oneself make sense. There can be a considerable increase in energy, effectiveness, and sense of fulfillment.

The change in Helen sounds easy, perhaps too easy. Here is an extract from her journal a few months later, when she had completed the course and moved several hundred miles to a remote part of Scotland.

> I love living on the Island. I love waking up every morning and looking out of my window at the sea and the breathtaking scenery. I am enjoying putting the house in order the boring homely things. I do fear everything in its place and me having nothing to do and no-where to go. This goes back to being useful. I am going to try and get a part time job at something I am trained for and try to give myself permission to do things just for me!!! Sitting watching the sea, I have been doing that

sometimes so my P is still in there fighting but my anxious J is fighting for survival. The J upbringing sees my future as having time lots of time with no useful obligations or chores to employ me resulting in masses of guilt. Meanwhile my new found liberated P is saying OK useful partly, and some time to partly have fun Do NOTHING Do anything.

I do sometimes wonder if the house will ever be sorted. My J side is having a nervous breakdown in almost every room, whilst the P is saying there is always tomorrow. I feel a little anxious at the moment because they are at war causing me inner conflict resulting in anxiety. Progress . . . at least I now know where my anxiety is coming from.

Thus, Helen's "new found liberated P" hasn't just replaced her J. She describes the two preferences as "at war," but she is also clear that this is progress.

Ryan (2001) describes a more troubled search for her type, illustrating the power of her upbringing (self-effacing, service-oriented Catholic in her case) and how the impact of one statement can change a life. The most valuable element of her article, though, is her analysis of verifying her type over *several* years: lots of reading, especially the picture of childhood for her type in the first edition of *Please Understand Me,* evaluating her experiences, and experimenting with behaving differently. For example, like Helen, she reduced the structure and formality of her life. The results were anxiety, increased energy, and improved moods, but she emphasizes the point that "dislocation" as a child made it extremely difficult for her to live as her true type. It was "an exercise in psychological contortion with ramifications for, and reverberations from, family and friends" (19).

UNDERSTANDING AND VALUING OTHERS

The second general aim is to increase understanding and valuing of other people, especially those who are our opposites in one or more preferences. This is what Isabel Myers meant by her phrase "the constructive use of difference." For example, someone who likes the "big picture" and therefore probably prefers Intuition can see those with the opposite preference as either narrow and pedestrian or, to put this more constructively and much more in tune with MBTI theory, as realistic and therefore valuable and interesting. At the least, we can be less likely to see people who are opposite in type to ourselves as odd, incompetent, malicious, or wrong.

The following example, like the one from Helen above, is partly about self-acceptance but also about someone with a preference for J reconsidering (and at this point probably overstating) her view of those who prefer P. Alicia is an INFJ writing with an ENFJ flavor in her journal after an introductory MBTI workshop.

> Exhale! Phew! What a relief it is to feel so understood. I am not Sad, Mad or Bad, and more importantly, I am not alone in my preferences. . . . Through the Myers-Briggs exercise I understand the influence of the "J" type preference in my interaction with others. I have often thought that those who behave opposite to me did so because they were in a relationship with me; that somehow I provoked an adverse reaction in them. You could say that at times, I have a kind of persecutory complex. I feel so relieved to have a theory that explains, "P-type" for instance, people whose behavior is often diametrically opposed to mine.
>
> It was very useful to hear that "P" types also have a sense of responsibility, but they just operate differently. Difference, that's what it all seems to hinge on. Not better or worse but different. This has helped me to put many things which I previously saw as problems into a new perspective. I know how alienated I feel when functioning in a way that is contrary. So I now appreciate that in expecting others to think and behave as I do would also alienate them from their true self. It will be very challenging for me to accept that in spite of the evidence to the contrary, Ps are just as reliable and just as committed as Js. Emm!

This sounds like a dramatic change. Did Alicia also *behave* differently? For example, another student, an ENFJ, used to dismiss introverts as dull and uninteresting. In an essay, she wrote that she is now inclined to see them as reflective and that she has changed her behavior—writing a note to an introverted colleague rather than "bouncing in without warning" to see her. Further questions concern how long such changes last, and whether other changes develop from them. More sophisticated evaluations of how far MBTI training and feedback achieve their aims need to measure changes in behavior as well as attitude.

Let's take a final example of a journal entry, again shortly after quite a long introductory workshop (about six hours of verifying MBTI results). Lucy decided quickly that she is an INTJ and has stayed with that decision and stayed very interested in the theory.

> Fantastic! All this MBTI stuff!! I'm a psychological type!!! And, naturally enough for my type, I'm fascinated by it (seeing patterns in external world!!) It is making me realise so much by it. My type is INTJ. It is a saddo type in one way—ivory tower stuff—but I like being an INTJ. It's very liberating to say—yes, that's what I am and somebody (or some type theory) has recognised the benefits of what I am. No doubt there's aloofness as a negative trait. There are wonderful things about being an INTJ. And I am glad to be inhabiting those things— its all part of inhabiting my skin and enjoying inhabiting it. In J's type theory I'm an EMED—Easily motivated, easily depressed, which makes me laugh. He is an INTP or an INFP. He thinks INFP (is this his ideal self?) we all think INTP. It's just struck me that ISTP was G.H, his friend. I'm glad to see J and I have some things in common—I and N and possibly T!! It is only the P that we row about—I don't have any other differences. Oh—perhaps that I'm more critical of others than he is. It explains why T and W annoy me—they are perhaps the exact opposite of me. Thinking about it I think J is an INFP.

This journal entry illustrates fulfillment of both the main aims of MBTI feedback, and I think is INTJ in style, with an FJ start. It includes a possible misinterpretation of theory—INTJs don't emphasize *external* patterns; it is very positive about being a (female) INTJ—"liberated" and perhaps vindicated and relieved; it recognizes some perceptions of herself by others, but gives them a subsidiary place; it compares MBTI theory favorably with another type theory; and characteristically J but not I, Lucy has quickly applied the theory to people she knows and to her relationships with them.

This is, of course, another example of an ideal outcome of MBTI feedback. In a systematic and balanced evaluation of training, negative accounts would also be gathered and analyzed.

EVALUATION OF TRAINING

There are two fundamental questions about MBTI feedback: "How often do positive changes happen as a result of MBTI feedback?" and "How often do unintended and undesirable consequences, such as an increase in stereotyping or a dislike of one's own type, happen?" These are not easy questions to answer, and to my knowledge there have been no systematic attempts to investigate them.

MBTI practice is not unusual in its lack of systematic and sophisticated evaluation. Most workshops, courses, and training programs are not rigorously evaluated, and Hinrichs's (1976) scathing remarks are still generally true. He wrote: "The good programme is attention-getting, dramatic, contemporary, or fun. Whether or not it changes behavior becomes secondary." Twenty-five years later, Salas and Cannon-Bowers (2001) recognize the problems of training evaluation, for example, that it's "costly, political and many times the bearer of bad news." They also see, however, "many thoughtful, innovative and practical approaches" and consider that its time is here, if only for the pragmatic reason that organizations want to know the return on their training investment. We need to understand good MBTI workshops and programs, apply the principles more widely, and evaluate using more than simple questionnaires in the last session ("happiness sheets").

The data gathered by Kise and Russell (2001) illustrate one qualitative approach. Kise worked in a middle school throughout a school year and collected many accounts of teachers' and students' experiences from interviews, observations, and student journals. The next step could be a more formal analysis of the data, a task made considerably easier by recent developments in computer analysis of text.

The three journal entries quoted in this chapter are all examples of *outcome* evaluation, in this case of the results of a substantial introductory workshop. However, such examples need to be representative. We also need *process* evaluation—assessing the training itself—but reports of process evaluations of MBTI workshops, courses, and programs have not been published.

The following information could be gathered:

1) Details of the participants

- age, etc.
- previous knowledge of the MBTI theory and questionnaire
- previous experience with personality measures and training

The information about the participants can tell the researcher whether the course works better for some groups of people than others.

2) Specific aims

The careful specification of aims can be quite a complex activity. For example, Merrill (1983) suggests ten types of learning on the basis of three "performance verbs" (remember, use, find) and four types of content (fact, concept, procedure, and principle). There are ten combinations in this model (because two of the twelve possible combinations do not exist, or so Merrill argues). Below are examples of aims that follow from the model:

Recall the sixteen types (Remember—fact).

Observe a preference systematically (Use—procedure).

3) Reactions of participants (enjoyment, perceived usefulness, and difficulties)

Decisions have to be made about when and how to gather this information. Interviews and questionnaires are the obvious ways. Some time, say a month, between training and evaluation is desirable. The key questions, at least at a skills level of evaluation, are what should participants be able to do after the training that they couldn't do before, and how well can they do it?

Patrick (1992, 2000) underlines the frequent neglect of training evaluation mentioned earlier. His view is that "There are many different methods and criteria advocated by different enthusiasts in the literature that makes evaluation potentially a confusing topic" (2000, 119), and he suggests four main approaches to evaluation. Only two of these are usually relevant to MBTI training. First, the conventional or traditional approach assesses participants' reactions, learning, and job performance (where relevant). In addition, it may be appropriate to measure aspects of organizational performance like absenteeism or production. Second, the effectiveness of elements of the training can be investigated, including the optimum amount of practice or the best design of an exercise.

ETHICAL USE OF MBTI THEORY

The major ethical problem in MBTI theory and practice is probably bias. It can be blatant or subtle, and can occur in anyone. For example, Hinnen (1994) analyzed *Gifts Differing* and argued that Isabel Myers overstated the qualities associated with I, N, and F. Some of his points are well argued, but others seem rather tenuous. For example, he sees defining S in one sentence and N in two longer sentences as evidence of bias; this could depend on how highly one values brevity.

Kummerow (2001) analyzed bias against the minority type in the Association of Psychological Type (APT), which is ESTJ in her reasoning, as the opposite of the majority type, though I suspect ISTP and ESTP are the least frequent. She used a five-stage model of cultural awareness. At the most aware stage—called Integration—the majority INFP culture explicitly values diversity: "We're all in it together; one way is not inherently better than another. To be liberated I must confront my own biases and stereotyping about ESTJs (and others)." At the same level, members of the minority ESTJ culture feel secure: "I am an ESTJ and offer much as a result of that. I also have much to learn from INFPs and other types" (8).

Kummerow wants to be practical and useful about this ethical problem, not because she's an ESTJ but "as an expression of my being an ESTJ." To her "because" sounds like stereotyping. I was doubtful about this at first. However, the key is explanation at the individual versus the group (and therefore stereotyping) level. It is the difference between saying or implying "I'm doing this because I'm a P and that tends to be the effect of P on me," and "I'm doing this because that's what Ps do." The implication in the latter statement is that *all* Ps do it, and *no* Js, and that's not what MBTI research has found.

The following example of "type-bashing" given by Kummerow is, I think, more straightforward. A plenary speaker at an international APT conference said she needed to explain an intuitive association/leap to people in the audience who were Sensing. Kummerow comments:

> Why single out sensing types? Did the intuitive types there make the same leap she did? . . . Why not just say something inclusive like, *"Let me explain my intuitive leap—many of you may have had your own."* Then the focus could have been on the fun of the association, not the alleged stupidity of sensing types for not leaping regularly. We don't need to exclude people with our comments; we simply need to recognize differences. Sensing types have an intuitive side, and intuitives have different intuitions from one another. (8)

Similarly, she suggests, we can say more inclusive things, like "This is an opportunity for everyone to use their introverted side" rather than "I know it will be hard for the Es to be quiet." That example is blatant stereotyping, but I find the sharpness of a similar statement about Js—that "Js moan"—appealing. What a confession! Kummerow's alternative seems to me too politically correct and too long: "Js may have an initial negative reaction when given new information on something they've already decided about" (8–9).

An alternative strategy, just as even-handed, would be to make negative statements equally about all the preferences, for example, Js tend to moan and Ps tend to dither. And I agree strongly with Kummerow's general argument that all MBTI users should review their language and try to be more inclusive.

Another example of these ethical problems around language is a U.K. advertisement for an organizational psychologist, which stated: "ESTJs and people who do not know what that means need not apply." This is a misuse of type theory, because the first part of the criterion discriminates unfairly against ESTJs. The best candidate might be any of the types, including ESTJ. If the job required primarily N and F skills, then a particular ESTJ might have developed those skills more than any of the other candidates, including those whose type actually includes N and F. Asking for knowledge of MBTI theory is a much more defensible criterion.

The different meanings of the same word for different types were discussed by Brock and Allen (2000). A further example is the term "concrete." One view is that it insults Ss. However, I think most terms can be misinterpreted and that concrete has a clear positive sense, as in the advice to writers in chapter 8. Take a more N term, "visionary," as another example. This can be flattering or—if it's seen as "great at ideas, but they're usually unrealistic and as for selecting and motivating staff, forget it"—highly critical. In management circles, the positive and negative interpretations can be a matter of fashion, but some will be consistently related to type: for example, perhaps Ns like to be called "visionary" more than Ss do. Some straightforward and useful research projects are implied.

Ethical Problem-Solving

Various frameworks have been proposed for resolving or at least clarifying ethical dilemmas. Bond (2000) recommends the following six steps designed to stimulate consideration of "as wide a range of options as possible before making a decision" (223).

1) Produce a brief description of the problem or dilemma.

Sometimes the dilemma will disappear. At other times, you will be in a better position to consult someone else.

2) Whose dilemma is it anyway? In what ways is it a problem for you or for others?

3) Consider all available ethical principles and guidelines. For MBTI theory and practice, there are several credible organizations with codes of ethics: the Myers and Briggs Foundation, CAPT, and APT. Other professional bodies each have their code or codes of ethics. Legal considerations are sometimes relevant too.

4) Identify all possible courses of action.

5) Select the best course of action.

6) Evaluate the outcome.

The issue for MBTI practice here is not with this framework, which seems ideal, but with applying it. Inevitably there will be ambiguous cases, or the best course of action will not be clear or will have unexpected consequences. I think we need to gather and analyze experience and gradually refine ethical understanding, in the way that other areas, like counseling, are doing.

Meanwhile, I agree with Lawrence and Martin (2001) that "ethical use and skillful use of the MBTI are the same thing" (175). They discuss stereotyping in detail, and analyze twelve stimulating ethics scenarios, giving their solutions, reasoning, and the ethical principles they drew on. The analyses are good illustrations of a basic principle in being ethical: that Codes of Ethics are guidelines and cannot reasonably be prescriptive. Being ethical is working through the kind of framework outlined above and, like other skills, develops with appropriate practice.

CONCLUSIONS

MBTI feedback appears to achieve its general aims of helping people understand and value themselves and others more, but virtually no systematic and rigorous evidence to support this conclusion has been published. Similarly, there are no published evaluations as far as I know of how well specific aims have been achieved. The increased emphasis on evaluation of training in organizations appears not to have affected MBTI workshops and consultancy. However, MBTI theory and practice should benefit if it does. There has been some relevant research on the process of verifying MBTI results, and this area is reviewed in the next chapter.

MBTI theory and practice have great potential for helping people but also for bias, blatant and subtle. To improve ethical use, the key issue is an educational one: developing and evaluating good training materials, guidelines, and examples.

Chapter 6

WHAT IS THE BEST APPROACH TO VERIFYING MBTI RESULTS?

T here are several approaches to helping people test the validity of their Myers Briggs Type Indicator® (MBTI®) results. We don't know yet how effective each is, and the answer may be complicated. It may depend on characteristics such as age, education level, and indeed type. For all the approaches, the spirit in which they are carried out is central: it should be one of open-minded inquiry, avoiding as far as possible the risk of premature closure. I discuss aspects of "setting the scene" and "atmosphere" in the section on using exercises.

This chapter is in two parts. The first part contains a discussion of seven issues in verifying type with groups in introductory workshops. The second part deals with giving feedback, with particular reference to one-to-one verifying of MBTI results, to Bathurst's (2000) research on bias in this context, and to strategies for clarifying type, treating it as detective work (Carr 1997).

SEVEN ISSUES IN VERIFYING TYPE WITH GROUPS

The seven issues involved in verifying type with groups are listed below:

- possible frameworks: the elements to include in the workshop and the best sequence for them
- reducing bias
- when to score the MBTI questionnaire (or, more fundamentally, should it be used?)

- when not to use it
- ambiguous results
- is everyone a type?
- using exercises: some suggestions, which need testing, on how exercises can be used most effectively

Possible Frameworks

Perhaps the most obvious and widely used framework for verifying MBTI results is to take each pair of preferences in turn and either talk about it, do one or more exercises to attempt to show it in action, or both. One question about this method is the order in which to take each preference. Should we follow the same order as the four-letter code or take Sensing–Intuition and Thinking–Feeling first, as Steve Myers does, because they are the "mental muscles" in his approach, and Extraversion-Introversion and Judging–Perceiving describe how the muscles are used (S. Myers 1995, 1997)? Or should we take J–P first (Bayne 1995), my usual approach, because I have found one J–P exercise to be the most likely of all the exercises to work and thus the best one to engage the group at the start.

Other frameworks may work better than taking each preference in turn, whatever the order. For example, temperament could be introduced first, as descriptions rather than in terms of the preference letters, before answering the MBTI questionnaire. It is also moving from the simple (four patterns) to the complex (sixteen patterns). A further possibility here would be to formally teach observation skills rather than just to suggest: "Try observing yourself over the next few days when you're (say) making decisions." The rationale would be to encourage an exploratory and investigative attitude and to increase self-awareness, and therefore increase the chance of valid MBTI results.

I investigated the related idea of people looking in a mirror while completing self-report questionnaires (Bayne 1988), which had achieved some excellent results in other research. I found that looking in the mirror didn't increase the accuracy of MBTI results; they were sufficiently accurate for there to be a ceiling effect, at least with the criterion of accuracy used and with that group of people.

A major strength of leaving the MBTI questionnaire (or the results) until later is that the results are treated as one of many pieces of evidence. On the other hand, if the questionnaire is completed first, it can be answered in a fresh way—an opportunity that comes only once at best. Moreover, MBTI results are sufficiently accurate to be useful: generally about 75 percent accurate for all four preferences, and over 90 percent accurate for three (Walck 1992; Myers et al. 1998, 116). Harvey (1996, 21–22) makes some useful suggestions for further studies on this issue.

Another issue is when to introduce details of MBTI theory. The *Manual* is very clear:"it is strongly recommended that respondents self-assess their preferences *prior* to being provided with the MBTI results" (Myers et al. 1998, 116, emphasis in original). However, I think this can be seen as biasing the exercises, and if the trainer describes the preferences so that the self-ratings can take place, she or he has an unnecessary chance to unintentionally speak in a biased way.

Another framework is to introduce type in several different ways in the same session. The underlying principle is that each approach works best for some people. Thompson (1999) in his "multiple-modality feedback system" (MMFS) uses several modalities, including cognitive, imagery, movement (kinesthetic), self-perception, and the perceptions of others. MBTI results represent the cognitive modality, and Thompson gives the results after the other steps. He begins with imagery, a technique he sees as "engaging the unconscious" (14), and with a separate exercise for each pair of preferences, followed by movement. Next, he asks participants to rate themselves on each pair of preferences, after brief explanations. I think this is less likely to be useful. It is very difficult not to bias the explanation; the preferences are subtle concepts, which cannot be defined with enough precision in a few words or a few anecdotes; and a major goal of the MBTI questionnaire is to avoid such problems. Next, participants are given a form—a rating scale for each preference—for people who know them well to complete. Overall, I consider the MMFS to be very rich and ingenious but too complicated.

A variation is to include other levels of MBTI theory or other elements or both, for example, the temperaments, interaction styles (Berens 2001), themes (Nardi 1999), and role-play (sketches) by those trainers who are dramatically inclined. The themes approach means presenting clients with a sixteen types matrix, ten themes per type. They cross some out and choose others; then they read the "snapshots" for those they've chosen. Each theme needs to be read as part of the larger pattern for that type. Following are some examples of the themes, which include some surprises:

1) For ENFP

   Inspiring and facilitating others

   Exploration of perceptions

   Finding the magical situation

2) For ISTJ

   Drawing up plans and being prepared

   Taking responsibility

   Doing the right thing

3) For ISFP

   Creative problem solving

   Building relationships

   Being their own true self

The larger pattern idea means for example that ENFPs' explorations tend to be of perceptions that may inspire others rather than of something more tangible. Overall, I think the themes approach is a sophisticated and potentially fruitful line of thought and investigation, but in its early stages and perhaps unnecessarily complicated. It is probably more suited to some psychological types than others, like the other elements and frameworks. Moreover, some of the themes do, at least in isolation rather than as a pattern, sound like Barnum statements.

Two other options are to introduce (1) the eight attitude functions, each with its own exercise (as in Thompson 1996a), and (2) the facets of the MBTI Step II—the concepts, not the questionnaire items. Because the facets are more specific, they are more recognizable and ask less of people's self-awareness. They also set the tone of "clues towards a decision" well, because most people have some subscales out of pattern. Jean Kummerow said in a Step II workshop that she'd asked a group to self-sort on all twenty facets (that is, twenty exercises) and that it worked. However, that requires a lot of patience. When I use this approach I use either the facet that correlates most highly with each preference, or the facet or facets that are most relevant to the particular group (for example, with students, pressure-prompted versus stress avoiding usually evokes a clear shock of recognition), or a mixture.

Jeffries (1991) asks, "Is there an ideal sequence of events when presenting a feedback session to a group of people?" (73). He answers, "Yes," and gives the following format:

1) Some general observations about type and the MBTI questionnaire

2) An overview of the eight preferences:

"This section is at the heart of the presentation. I routinely discuss the eight preferences for about two hours, grounding the entire time in anecdotes" (74)

3) Return participants' MBTI results

4) Exercises

5) Type table

6) More input

7) Warnings

In marked contrast to Jeffries, I prefer to introduce the MBTI theory and questionnaire and myself very briefly; respond to any wariness about questionnaires, psychologists, and so on; do an exercise; and then either give out the MBTI questionnaire or, if completed beforehand, ask the group members to score their own. Then, after scoring but before participants know what the letters or combinations of letters mean, I ask them to do two or more exercises. The first exercise is a type table, to help me choose which other exercises to use. Most exercises need at least three people with each preference, though there are ways round this, described in the section on using exercises.

The main general advantages of this very different sequence and approach are, first, that the outcomes of the exercises cannot be biased by information about type, and second, that it is much more participative than a two-hour overview with lots of anecdotes. Indeed, I have no wish to tell lots of anecdotes once, let alone "hundreds of times" (Jeffries 1991, 57). I use at most one or two anecdotes after the exercises, if they seem needed. This is partly because I do not remember or much like telling anecdotes and partly because I would rather the group do the exercises, see the differences when they happen, and come up with their own examples. This may also reduce the chance of unintentional and perhaps nonverbal bias in referring to each preference, temperament, or type.

Reducing Bias

Bias may be more likely in some of the frameworks than others. Some general strategies for reducing it were discussed in chapter 5. Another strategy was suggested by Steve Myers (personal communication, 2003). For a few years, he's been introducing the idea of type bias to groups by saying, "we all do it," and inviting groups to "pull him up."

He has found the results frightening because he has discovered that he is more biased than he'd realized. I think this is a very promising strategy.

When to Score the MBTI Questionnaire

Kroeger's view on scoring the MBTI questionnaire, expressed in a 1991 workshop on designing a day, is that it is unprofessional for people to score their own. He argued that consultants are not paid to watch people fill in questionnaires, that the error rate for self-scoring is high, and that the trainer should always know the group's type table beforehand, and that, ideally, the trainer should examine the answer sheets.

I think these are good arguments, but that the arguments for my approach outlined above have value too. There is more "ownership of the data" if people complete their questionnaires in the workshop. It means I can respond to any problems or queries. They also seem to enjoy learning the scoring, and the scoring keys are beautifully designed. I do the scoring as a cascade; that is, I show the first four people to finish how to use the scoring keys on their own answer sheets, and they show the others as they finish, while I supervise. I look at each set of results to see if it looks likely (I typically work with groups of twenty to thirty). If it looks suspect, I rescore it myself, tactfully.

With students (psychology and counseling), I have found it essential when they are scoring their own answer sheets to say, firmly, something like "Some people tend to go straight in and not to read instructions. Please have a go at reading them *one at a time* and doing *each one in turn*." This only works with some people! I go round, of course, and check/help. The one-on-one contact also contributes to the atmosphere. I share Otto Kroeger's dislike of the self-scoring version of the MBTI questionnaire.

I am arguing here for more room for diversity in introducing type to groups. I agree with Bill Jeffries when he writes, "you will find a style that best suits you" (79), but not when he adds, "You also, no doubt, will begin to collect stories and examples," and not with his "ideal sequence." And I agree with and am helped by Otto Kroeger when he says, "Never do dominant and auxiliary in a one-day or less session" and "Always underkill," but not when he says, "Always know your type table beforehand."

When *Not* to Use the MBTI Questionnaire

Suggestions include the following:

- When trust is low
- When literacy may be low
- When a previous negative experience with type, or with an approach the person or group sees as similar, hasn't been sufficiently resolved
- When the context is unethical, for example, when MBTI results are likely to be misused
- When stress levels are very high

Ambiguous Results

Ambiguous results—when someone is unsure about the accuracy of MBTI results—are most likely to happen with low scores (say, less than ten) and for one or two pairs of preferences rather than three or four. However, they do happen with very clear scores and for all four pairs of preferences. Several factors can be the crucial explanation for a particular person's results, and it would be useful to know how likely each one is, both for theory and applications. The following are possible explanations for ambiguous results:

1) Faking. The person *deliberately* answered the MBTI questionnaire as an ideal person, parent, or applicant rather than honestly. How the MBTI questionnaire was introduced and the context may well be influential here.

2) Lack of self-awareness about one or more of the preferences.

3) Problems with type development. One or more of the person's true preferences have not developed sufficiently. She or he does not behave most of the time in harmony with the preferences, so answers honestly but inaccurately. MBTI theory suggests tension—being pulled one way and then the other—and other side effects as a result.

4) Development of the person's third or fourth function is a current priority, either deliberately or as part of individuation.

5) Misunderstanding of the meaning of one or more of the pairs of preferences.

6) Severe stress. The person answered "in the grip."

7) Type theory does not apply to this person. She or he genuinely

does not have a particular preference or preferences. This is the "No personality theory is perfect" factor, also discussed from a different angle in the next section: is everyone a type?

8) The person completed the MBTI questionnaire carelessly or randomly.

Because MBTI results are—or at least appear to be—generally valid, none of the factors will occur often. The research findings with the NEO-PI are also good evidence for the value and accuracy of quite transparent measures (McCrae and Costa 1983; Funder 1999). Multiple perspectives, as in some of the strategies reviewed in this chapter, will counter, explore, and perhaps resolve ambiguous issues. Greater clarity about each explanation should, nevertheless, allow more effective choice of strategies and the decision, made with the other person, about when to stop.

Is Everyone a Type?

MBTI theory seems to me to assume that everyone is a type and that therefore strategies for clarifying type apply. However, a pragmatic and respectful approach is to accept the possibility that a few people are genuinely versatile, or equally comfortable with both of one or more preferences. It would be useful to know the proportion of people for whom this is true with each preference, and why they have this flexibility (rather than tension) and presumably greater balance.

Some people don't experience themselves as a type and some don't behave in ways consistent with a type. Quenk and Mitchell (1997) suggested three perspectives on this issue: clinical experience, theoretical (Jungian) considerations, and empirical evidence. Garden (1991, 7–9) also gave a clear analysis of Jung's view of this question. Genuine and comfortable flexibility seems to be quite rare, and MBTI theory would need to adjust only slightly to include it. Part of the idea of a prototype, discussed briefly in chapter 2, is that some people can belong in two or more categories. The obvious problem is at the level of type dynamics and personality structure: the person would have two dominant functions (and presumably two fourth functions, and so on). A case study approach should be illuminating on this issue, exploring comfort versus tension and developmental aspects in particular.

Using Exercises

Exercises are experiential activities used to illustrate or test aspects of

MBTI theory. The general principles for using an exercise are to (1) try an exercise out on yourself first, (2) set the scene, and (3) to discuss the outcomes fully. Setting the scene is about the atmosphere, which in turn is affected most by trust. It may be mainly conveyed nonverbally. I find it helpful to say something like, "Type may sound as if it's putting people into boxes. It isn't, it's a *step toward* understanding individuality." That's part of the general scene setting. The exercises themselves can be introduced as *"usually working"* and "I'll put you into different groups for each exercise but the MBTI results are *indications* so if you'd like to see what it's like in another group during an exercise, I'd like you to do it."

I'm inclined to rush through the discussion after an exercise, but I'm learning to be more measured and thorough. It's good practice to ask such questions as: "Does this relate to any problems you/the group have at work?" and "Does this explain any of your reactions (to each other)?" With some groups, perhaps all groups, it's usually best to relate the workshop to their concerns and interests at the start. Then the discussion following the exercises can be structured accordingly. For example, a structure could be

1) What happened?

2) What do you think and feel about what happened during the exercise (and now)?

3) Any conclusions?

4) Any implications? Some participants will appreciate a related action plan.

There's lots of scope for exploring what's really going on and relating it to familiar situations. More, or less, structure than this may appeal, however.

Sometimes the exercises don't work, which can be worrying. When that happens, I remember Otto Kroeger's advice, in a workshop on running workshops, to "trust the process" and to ask the group how they went about the exercise (Bayne 1995, 149). This can be at least as revealing as the obvious outcome. Indeed, I quite often ask for comments on the group process to be written on the newsprint, too—then it becomes part of the outcome as well as a safety net. In any case, the most important aspect of the exercise is that people learn about the particular difference, so that they can verify their types accurately in due course if they wish. Another strategy here is to have results from the same exercise with another group in reserve: "This is what should have happened!"

Some of the workshop members may be content to act as observers—perhaps those who are unsure about a particular exercise. Usually there are striking differences between, say, a T and an F group given exactly the same task. An alternative here is the "fish bowl," with at least as many observers as central participants, and usually more. I find it very useful with pair-preference exercises to use the clarity index to form the groups. I ask the whole group to form a line, or a U shape or series of groups if the room is small, so that people with high scores on, say, E are at one end, those with high scores on I at the other, and those with low scores toward the middle, in order. Then I go along the line trying to form the groups at natural breaks. Using the clarity index to form groups could look as if a trait model is being used; however, groups are formed quickly, and I think the benefits are greater than this possible problem.

A follow-up to the preference exercises is to ask each group to discuss and report back on one or more of the following:

- three (say) questions they'd like to ask the other group
- what they value most about their own preference
- what they value most about the opposite preference (and therefore, generally speaking, the other group)

Several examples of exercises are discussed in the next chapter, chosen because I've used them successfully or think they're promising. They're also simple in format. For other exercises, and other kinds of exercise, for various groups including high school students and managers, see Hirsh (1992), Kroeger and Thuesen (1988, 1992, 1994), Marlowe (1998), Abella and Dutton (1995), Hayman and Allen (1997), Fields and Reid (1999), and Lawrence and Martin (2001).

VERIFYING TYPE ONE-TO-ONE

All the strategies used with groups can be used one-to-one, but with two major drawbacks. First, there is much less chance to see type in action. Second, if Bathurst's views and data (discussed next) are accurate and generally true, there is considerable unintended bias in one-to-one feedback and presumably less bias in a group.

In a very large sample of 21,000 people, Bathurst (2000) found a correlation between the type of the administrator (the person giving feedback on MBTI results) and the client. He also found that best fit and MBTI types agreed only 50 percent of the time, which compares badly with the 75 percent accuracy in this best fit type sense reported in Myers et al. (1998). The two findings may well explain each other. On closer analysis, Bathurst found that administrators with a preference for Sensing produced more changes from Intuition to Sensing and administrators with a preference for Intuition the opposite, and administrators with a preference for Feeling produced more changes from Thinking to Feeling. This may be worth investigating further: what is it that the administrators tend to do, and how can it be reduced? An obvious response would be to develop a greater understanding of what goes on in a one-to-one feedback session, building on what is already known about accuracy and biases in person perception (Bayne 1995; Funder 1999).

However, I think the best solution probably lies in materials and training, and that Carr (1997), writing about type clarification, is an excellent resource in both respects. First, she is clear, relevant, and succinct about the theory, for example, "Type clarification is a sifting process, in which the practitioner tries to help the client to isolate their basic, enduring preferences from other influences on their behavior" (2). Second, she discusses the process of verifying, cautioning for example that "we need to ensure that the exploration process is driven by the client's desire for clarity rather than our own" (4), and "avoid using single 'deciding' examples." On the second of these, I'd go further and say that several examples are needed, perhaps in a ratio of three pointing toward one preference and none toward its opposite. (The ratio of 3:0 is based on studies of accuracy in judging personality characteristics, emotional states, and moods).

The rest of the booklet discusses strategies and techniques. The first is called "opening questions," for example, "What do you see in yourself that leads you to say you could be either?," which can economically reveal that the person's uncertainty is simply a misunderstanding of what one or more of the preferences means in MBTI theory. The other techniques are exploration of "shoulds," "musts," and "oughts"; investigation of different situations and times (periods of the person's life); investigating implications of type dynamics and development (including Step II and reactions to extreme stress); observing behavior; and trying a type out for a few hours or days. The only missing strategy

I can think of is temperament theory. Some people might also quarrel with the inclusion of the MBTI Step II under type dynamics when the two approaches are fundamentally different and indeed in some respects antagonistic.

Carr also includes three longer case examples, including her own: ESTP or ENTP? The only comment that I found jarring was that feedback from others is "likely to be especially useful for people whose level of self-awareness is relatively low" (13). I think this is wrongly and unnecessarily critical of people who find this strategy useful, and that it oversimplifies the patchy nature of self-awareness. There are also several cartoons, and my favorite was in this section. A teacher with a superior air asks a bewildered class: "So I'd like you to ask yourself: are you one of them—loud, intrusive, superficial—or one of us—calm, thoughtful and deep!"

CONCLUSIONS

Approaches to verifying type should be evaluated more, and more rigorously. However, it is not practical either in time or cost to evaluate each approach. There are far too many elements and sequences of them, and in any case the outcome would probably be the same as in counseling research: most of the frameworks would work about equally well. What is probably most practical and desirable is to focus on particular aspects of verifying, for example, on the effectiveness of an attempt to reduce bias in presentation or on particular exercises.

Chapter 7

WHICH ARE THE BEST EXERCISES AND TYPE DESCRIPTIONS?

 n this chapter, I first review and analyze exercises for verifying (testing) Myers Briggs Type Indicator® (MBTI®) results in introductory groups, taking each preference in turn. The assumption that this is the most effective approach was discussed in chapter 6, as were aspects of the skills of using exercises. Then I discuss several attempts at describing the psychological types, with particular attention to the problem of Barnum statements.

EXTRAVERSION–INTROVERSION EXERCISES

I have seen fewer exercises for E-I than for the other preferences, perhaps because it is the most familiar concept and in everyday use, and therefore tends to be taken for granted.

The following two work fairly well for me:

1) Divide into E and I groups. Ask them to discuss the topic, "When you see someone you'd like to know better, what do you do?"

Good outcome. The Es, particularly the highest scoring Es, agree that they take fairly direct action such as going up to the attractive person. The Is look aghast and say there is no way they would do that. Rather, they may try nonverbal signals—essentially "flirting"—and hope the other person approaches them.

I don't think it matters in this exercise which group reports back first. The main caution is to emphasize the broader conception of E-I in type theory than in most other theories.

Variation. You go to a party where you know only the host. What do you do?

2) Divide the group on E–I (and J–P if it's a large group), and ask them to discuss, and see to what extent they agree on, how they go about writing an essay or report from the start.

Good outcome. IJs tend to plan visits to the library and anticipate lots of reading and note-taking. IPs tend to put the task aside until the deadline is near, but meanwhile notice references, ideas, news items, and so on. EJs want to discuss it and begin writing. EPs tend to put it aside until the deadline is near; there are lots of other things to do first.

This exercise is better than the first in its illustration of E–I as direction of energy rather than the narrower conception of how sociable or gregarious someone is. Observers can be useful for both exercises. Usually they report that the E group is louder and more expressive.

SENSING–INTUITION EXERCISES

There are four main kinds of exercise for S–N so far: Describe or talk about an everyday object; describe a picture, photo, or event after seeing it briefly; draw a map/give instructions; describe an abstract quality.

Everyday Object

Examples: cup, tea bag, telephone, the room you're in, the sea, a piece of fruit, a spring day, a Christmas tree. More concrete if the object is actually in the room, even more if each group has one.

Proviso: The object needs to be either very familiar to all the group or actually in the room.

Instructions. Divide into S and N groups (or further divisions using type dynamics or J–P if it's a large group). Write about your group's agreed description of this object on a piece of newsprint. You have about five minutes.

The actual words in the instructions used may be crucial. "Write about x" or "Talk about x" have both worked for me.

Good Outcome. Ss describe in detail giving real, factual information; Ns give uses, free associations, mental leaps, links, and metaphors. Ss are also more likely to count, for example, the number of chairs in the room.

Variation. (1) Consider asking for an example when an obvious word is used—each group may be using it quite differently. (2) Ask the whole group to describe the object in a sensing way and then in an intuitive way. Ask them to observe how comfortable it was to use each function. (3) People can write their responses individually first and compare within their S or N groups before reporting back to the whole group.

Picture, Photo, or Event

Examples: A Dali, an advertisement, a short film, a trainer behaving unusually.

Comment: I've tried several of Dali's paintings, and they only work well sometimes. The task of answering questions on a film or after a trainer has behaved unusually is obviously related to research on eyewitness reports in forensic psychology. The general finding in eyewitness research is that people are not accurate, which is surprising in view of the high proportion of Ss in the general population. No one as far as I know has compared Ss and Ns on their accuracy as eyewitnesses, but in any case this approach to S-N exercises may be unnecessarily elaborate.

Variation: Broer and McCarley (1999) tried asking S and N volunteers to leave the room, then come back one at a time to answer observational questions with their backs to the group, for example, how many people in the room are wearing glasses, what color is Patricia's dress? The exercise didn't work in China, and Broer and McCarley think this is because the Chinese educational system's emphasis at that time on rote learning has a marked effect on development of S.

What criteria does a picture or photo need to meet for an S-N exercise to work? Cauvin and Cailloux (1999) suggested that it must be original or attractive to hold attention; have both numerous details and be evocative; and be unlikely to provoke strong value judgments. In their research, they showed a photo of a quay (reproduced in their article) for 30 seconds and then used a neutral phrase: "What can you say about the photo you have just seen?" They asked for an oral and a visual report from each group, keeping the instructions deliberately vague. They remark that "Participants will often ask for further explanation, which should not be given" (30) and recommend remembering who asks questions as possible material for later discussion.

In their experience, about ten minutes is the right length of time, or the S groups may evolve "from analysis to synthesis" and the Ns "from general impressions to justifying details." Their order for analysis is presentation without questions or comments; remarks by participants; reports by observers (if any); comments by the group leader.

Good outcome. In Cauvin and Cailloux's experience, Ns "always" show a simpler and more symbolic drawing than Ss, whose drawing is more realistic and more directly based on their observations. In their oral report, the Ss "very often" distinguish between what they have seen and their interpretations, and this reflects their approach to the exercise—an automatic emphasis on observation. The Ns generally start in the same way but quickly start talking about quite different things. They also usually start with an expression like "overall" or "our impression."

Another variation. For Harrison (1998), the following exercise is the "single most effective way I have found to dispel doubts about type theory" (39). After introductions she gives easel sheets (newsprint in the U.K.) and at least four colored markers to ST, SF, NT, and NF or IS, ES, IN, and EN groups. Then she asks them to plan and report an imaginary but realistic event or task such as a one-day school trip for a group of teachers or an induction day for a group of managers. She gives them fifteen to twenty minutes, after which the easels are presented one at a time.

Good Outcome. For Ss: usually one color, sequence of points, definite timings, usually a title, specific directions. Drawings are rare.

For Ns: usually three or more colors, seldom a sequence, either general timings or none, not usually titled, vague directions, drawings.

Comment. In Harrison's experience, this exercise always works, though presumably it wouldn't in China. In addition, I think her analysis supports the MBTI theory focus on S and N rather than on the function attitudes. The exercise sounds more J-P than S-N at first, but she comments that "other factors such as the number of Fs or Ps in the group may result in a less complete easel, but nevertheless the products are similar" (44).

Map/Instructions/Journey

Examples: the layout of the building you're in (from memory); the route from, say, London to Aberdeen or Washington, D.C., to New York City.

Outcome. I gave subgroups within 6 Ss (3 SPs) and 17 Ns two or three minutes to draw a map of the group floor of a quite complicated building, with a courtyard in the middle. The ENFPs included rabbits and trees (both real, though the rabbits weren't actually there at the time of drawing). The INxJs produced the most hushed moment with a simple, elegant, abstract, and schematic "map" of just a few straight lines, and the S group the most realistic and to scale. One participant considered that his N group had produced a very precise map, but then the S group pointed out numerous errors!

Variations. The groups tour the building to draw the layout. On reflection, this variation might give purer results because it has more to do with observation and does not involve memory of an introverted sensing kind as well. Another variation is to ask volunteers to leave the room and come back one at a time to give directions to somewhere nearby that is familiar to most of the group. Again, this should present S skills positively.

Abstract Quality

Example: time

Comment: Kroeger and Thuesen (1988, 90-91) give examples. Generally, Ns write more and use more abstract words, but my favorite was a group who wrote one word: "sand." This is quite a reliable exercise but my experience so far is that tea bags and apples work best.

THINKING–FEELING EXERCISES

There seem to be two main kinds of exercise for T–F: asking for a definition and asking for reactions to a situation.

Definition

Examples: love, conflict, power.

Divide the group into Ts and Fs. This exercise might work well for temperament groups too. Ask the groups to discuss and come up with a definition for X.

Good outcome. The T group(s) produce a more objective, cooler *definition,* the F group(s) some reactions, which are often emotional. For example, their reaction to "conflict" may be that they "find it very difficult." Observers usually report marked differences in group process: the Ts tend to debate, the Fs to share views more gently; the Ts are more likely to argue about which words to leave out, the Fs to include all the words.

Situation

Divide the groups into Ts and Fs. Ask them to discuss their reactions to "walking in a wood and finding an injured animal."

Good outcome. The Ts tend to be more objective and practical, and therefore kinder in a sense. Obviously experience can play a greater role here than in some exercises.

A variation would be to use a photograph or picture of people, as in some of the S–N exercises.

Another exercise is to ask T and F groups "Under what circumstances would you apologize?" and "How would you expect the other person to respond?"

Good outcome. Ts say they tend to apologize when they're wrong, and that they expect the other person to accept their apology. Fs tend to apologize when something has gone wrong or when someone is hurt or unhappy, as an expression of sympathy. They expect the other person to apologize in return.

The different meanings of *sorry* for Ts and Fs seem to be related to different philosophies, as discussed in chapter 8, in the section on feedback. However, it may be too influenced by social norms to be a reliable exercise. Saying sorry has been advocated as a useful management tool, for example, a public relations ploy. Perhaps the focus of the exercise should be on motives and beliefs. Apologies are deeply ambiguous so asking for a definition of a good apology could be effective. I can imagine T groups coming up with a list of, say, "appropriate, sparing, genuine (of course), convincing, with intent to rectify the mistake. . . ."

Another promising possibility is to ask the groups to select from sayings, like the "pot-shots" in Murray (1995). A more tested approach is to ask T and F groups to discuss such questions as how they like to be appreciated, what they like to be appreciated for, and what happens when they're not appreciated (discussed by Lawrence and Martin 2001, 224–25).

JUDGING–PERCEIVING EXERCISES

The following exercise has proved to be so reliable and compelling, at least with the groups I work with, that I usually use it as the first exercise (after handedness and a type table):

Instructions. (1) Organize groups of four to six people, separating high and low scorers on J, and high and low scorers on P. (2) Give a large sheet of paper and pens to each group. (3) Give to all groups the task of answering the question: "What is really important about plans and planning?" They have about five minutes to write down the things they agree on as a group, on the large sheet of paper.

Good outcome. The high J group set about the task with energy; they see lots of important things about plans, and they focus on the task. Their sheet of paper cites many qualities, including "clear," "achievable," "prioritized." The outcome for the high P group is, of course, in marked contrast. The purest outcome, which happens, is that they discuss the task in a desultory way and present a blank sheet at the end.

Low J and low P groups tend to produce more mixed results, though generally illustrating their respective preferences.

Variations. I first tried this exercise with the terms *goals* and *goal-setting.* One Perceiving group had been taught the characteristics of good goals and dutifully repeated them. However, the levels of energy were different: trust the process.

Steve Myers (personal communication, 2003) has tried two other variations: First, "What are the most stressful aspects of making or following plans? Rank them in order of stress." He emphasizes putting the stressful aspects in order and has found, for example, that J groups tend to put "Not meeting deadlines" and "Getting it wrong" first, and P groups "Making plans," "Following plans," and "Tracking plans." His second variation is to ask each group to describe what they think a plan entails. He finds that when the P group describe a plan, the J group are often shaking their heads and discounting the Ps' definitions, saying such things as "That isn't a plan" or asking "How can you guarantee that it is going to be met?"

Another J–P exercise is to ask J groups and P groups (or temperament groups) to devise a poster advertising an event.

Good outcome. J posters tend to include dates and times. P posters tend to be less organized. Again, comments by each group on the other group's poster can be illuminating but may need to be framed sensitively by the trainer.

DESCRIPTIONS OF THE TYPES

All introductory books on MBTI theory and applications include descriptions of the preferences and of various levels of type. The standard and most widely used descriptions are in the report form. Considerable effort was put into avoiding negative or biased language in the report form descriptions (Lawrence and Martin 2001, 179–80), but MBTI descriptions also have a "twist" (Bayne 1995), which, in general terms, is that strengths have corresponding weaknesses.

MBTI theory offers a useful perspective on the problem of words. For example, Allen and Brock (2000) found that "honest" was used to define an aspect of good communication by people in general, but when clarified actually meant quite different things to different types. For STs it tended to mean being given all the facts directly, and for NFs being listened to with genuine care and warmth.

Some central terms in MBTI theory are obviously open to abuse as well as to different interpretations, for example, "type" itself, Thinking, Feeling, and Judging—though Sensing, which seems a relatively neutral term, may, at MBTI conferences and in the MBTI literature, be the most misused word of all. One solution is to coin new words, but then each new word had to be defined using familiar words. I think the best solution is to say that terms like Sensing are technical terms and to use them carefully and ethically.

The most ambitious attempt at describing each type so far is by Berens and Nardi (1999). They offer three formats: brief "snapshot," third person, and first person. The first person portraits are composites from interviews with at least four people of each type. Berens and Nardi recommend considering all three formats together and find that each works best for some people. This seems to me a significant attempt to improve descriptions of the types, and one that in the self-portraits is partly empirical. However, it would be useful to know as with all the other descriptions which aspects of their snapshots, portraits, and self-portraits work best generally and which with particular kinds of people. In addition, there are some *possible* Barnum statements— descriptions of aspects of personality that seem individual but are actually true of most people—in the Berens and Nardi descriptions, such as "They often instantly like people or not" and "They often feel a strong need to discover a definitive direction for themselves" (both ENFP, 40). Research on Barnum statements is discussed in the next section.

An approach that has not been systematically tried yet would be to ask samples of five to ten participants of each type to describe their experience of each function. For example, ISFPs and ESTJs would both describe introverted Feeling, but as a dominant function and as the last of the eight respectively, at least according to the most complex version of type dynamics. It may be that the clearest descriptions of a preference, or of elements of it, would come from types for whom it is not the dominant or auxiliary. Type development would need to be taken into account.

Descriptions of each preference and to a lesser extent of each type are one of the most researched aspects of MBTI theory, for example, Ware and Yokomoto (1985), McCarley and Carskadon (1986) and Thorne and Gough (1991), and are discussed in Bayne (1995), Ruhl and Rodgers (1992), Pearman and Fleenor (1996), Harker et al. (1998), and Reynierse and Harker (2001a,b). The results of these studies need to be evaluated, and when they seem reliable and valid, compared with the descriptions used by practitioners.

We also need more rigorous evaluations of the type descriptions published in texts, to try to clarify which work best and then which elements of them work best (McCarley and Carskadon 1987). Among the descriptions with particularly good reputations are those in Brownsword (1987), Kroeger and Thuesen (1988), Hirsh and Kummerow (1989), especially the sections on each type's childhood, DiTiberio and Hammer (1993), Murray (1995), Lawrence (1998), and the early editions of Myers's *Introduction to Type* (e.g., 1976; reprinted in Lawrence 1993).

At least three attempts at developing rigorously evaluated descriptions have been made. First, the descriptions in *Introduction to Type,* in various editions, have been tested. Second, Pearman and Albritton (1997) included only descriptions that had appeared in three different studies, at least in the set of descriptions on pages 32–39. Third, the descriptions in the sixth edition of *Introduction to Type,* revised by Linda Kirby and Katharine Myers, are empirically based in a very thorough way (Myers et al. 1998, 119), and seem to me to set the standard (Bayne 2004).

Format of description could also be investigated. For example, the Mental Muscle Diagram (S. Myers 1995, 1997) and the type chart designed by Marlowe (1998) have a visual impact that is notably unrestrictive while Lawrence (1998) arranged his descriptions with opposite types on the same page. Also, we may need to evaluate descriptions for different levels of knowledge of MBTI theory, ages (or type development), cultures and kinds of use, and for emphasis on motives or behavior. Lawrence's (1998) descriptions "emphasize the values and priorities of the types . . . because they are the motivational energy behind the behaviors."

The conclusions and recommendations made by McCarley and Carskadon (1987), and summarized here, are still very pertinent fifteen years later:

1) Some type descriptions are rated much higher than others

2) No one theorist seems superior as a source of descriptions

3) Separate descriptions for men and women don't seem to be needed

4) The descriptions of Sensing did not seem to be stereotypical

5) Overall, the descriptions studied were "fairly high" in accuracy but could be "substantially improved" (10) by modifying them on the basis of empirical research.

McCarley and Carskadon give a stimulating example of the kind of description that could result. It combines descriptors from two theorists (Myers and Keirsey); those elements likely to be seen as most accurate are presented first; and each descriptor includes a probability statement, for example, "almost all ENFPs are very enthusiastic (96%)" and "ENFPs sometimes suffer from muscle tension (57%)" (13). One of McCarley and Carskadon's methodological concerns is discussed next: detecting Barnum descriptions.

BARNUM STATEMENTS

Most researchers in this area have been interested in how gullible people are when rating descriptions of their own personalities. Some have been trying to explain the success of astrology and other fringe techniques. Most studies of Barnum statements go through the following stages:

1) A personality technique, usually a paper-and-pencil test, is completed by a group of participants.

2) The test is apparently scored by the experimenter.

3) Exactly the same results, a set of Barnum statements, are given to each participant.

4) The participants rate the descriptions on accuracy, and rate the technique on effectiveness.

In research on astrology, a variation of this design is to send clients descriptions drawn up on the wrong birth data. Because astrology descriptions tend to include Barnum statements, the effect is the same: generally, the descriptions are rated as highly accurate and the technique as very effective.

The finding demonstrates clearly that asking people about the accuracy of their results is not a safe way of evaluating the validity of a technique for measuring personality. The Barnum statements tend not to be useful for describing individuality or even type; they are fairly general truths about people (or at least people in a particular time and culture) masquerading as insights into an individual's personality.

Below are examples of Barnum statements, with some analysis:

1) *Security is one of your major goals in life.* The "one of " is significant here, because it makes the statement more vague and easier to agree with. From an MBTI theory point of view, though, this statement should seem less of an insight to SPs, NTs, and NFs than to SJs.

2) *You have found it unwise to be too frank in revealing yourself to others.* "Too frank" begs the question, to some extent. However, NFs with their emphasis on authenticity might disagree more than other temperaments, and Extraverts more than Introverts (or Is more than Es?).

3) *You have a great need for other people to like and admire you.* MBTI theory would predict this to be true of Fs more than Ts. The term "great" in this Barnum statement seems less vague.

Indeed, more concrete and individual versions of the Barnum statements discovered so far may also be worth trying out. Several of the other Barnum statements that, by definition, most people rate as accurate about themselves would also be predicted by MBTI theory to be more true of some types than others. For the original list, used often since, see Forer (1949) or Bayne (1995).

The Barnum effect is influenced by several factors (Furnham and Schofield 1987). An important one is that the feedback is predominantly positive in tone, which of course is deliberately true of MBTI feedback, particularly early on. Forer's experimental design, used often since, though with variations such as using genuine feedback, more sensitive questioning, and more powerful statistics (Furnham and Schofield, 1987), can probably be simplified. I think asking people to rate how true each statement is of (1) themselves, (2) two people they know well, and (3) most people, might be enough.

The main issue for MBTI practice is to test the numerous type, temperament, other pairs, and preference descriptions for Barnum statements. They would then be deleted or modified because they are not revealing about an individual's personality and give a misplaced sense of confidence in descriptions that include them. It can be too comfortable, and an illusion. On the other hand, confidence—misplaced or not—can be therapeutic!

CONCLUSIONS

More analyses of exercises, as in Harrison (1998) and Cauvin and Cailloux (1999), would be very valuable for MBTI theory and practice. For example, they can contribute to understanding of the core meaning of the preferences and to ideas about the best clues for observing type accurately. I think the exercises also need to be evaluated more formally.

The many descriptions of the preferences and types need further evaluation. Berens and Nardi (1999) is a novel and partly empirical attempt that deserves priority in my view, but the large-scale studies also need to be further evaluated and, where appropriate, applied. The clear methods described by McCarley and Carskadon (1987) and in the *Manual*, or a variation of them, should be used to evaluate the other descriptions.

Chapter 8

APPLYING MBTI THEORY
TO COMMUNICATION

I n this chapter, I first discuss two approaches to the different "languages" thought to be spoken by the types: those of Brock and Thompson. Then I review some applications of Myers Briggs Type Indicator® (MBTI®) theory to writing, to giving feedback (in interviewer training and on essays), to receiving feedback, and to empathy and listening. Finally, an exercise on empathy and listening is described and analyzed.

Two general perspectives on good communications are widely accepted by MBTI practitioners: that it can be very helpful (1) to know your own type's communication strengths and blind spots, and (2) to recognize other types' radically different strengths and blind spots. Two implications are that the people we find it easier to communicate with are usually those of the same or a similar type, and that if we wish to communicate more effectively, we can adapt our responses—or at least learn to adapt them.

BROCK'S APPROACH TO COMMUNICATION

Brock (1994) calls adapting to another person "flexing" and developed the FLEX™ model of communication (Allen and Brock 2000), which when applied to the health professions is called FLEX™ Care. In Brock's view, it is easier to observe the person's current "language" or mode than their psychological type, and good communication usually means flexing—matching the other person's language.

Allen and Brock suggest three possible general options in each interaction:

1) to see the other person as wrong and feel critical of him or her,

2) to see yourself as wrong and criticize yourself, or

3) to see the two of you as different but equally OK.

Obviously, it is the last option that is a major application of MBTI theory, and Allen and Brock (2000) analyze several examples of interactions insightfully and sharply.

As an example of a general finding, let's take nurses with a Feeling preference who tend to experience particular difficulty with patients in a Thinking mode. These nurses can see patients in this mode as distant and impersonal and can feel rebuffed and de-skilled as a result. MBTI theory reframes this situation as "Patients using their Thinking may not want to express their emotions at that time but may well do so at their own pace. What they probably want first from you is acceptance of their initial, detached reaction." The Feeling nurse may be able to flex to a Thinking mode (and feel empathic and skillful doing so) while being ready for any change in the patient's mode.

Knowledge of one's own type is very relevant in this kind of situation. In MBTI theory, Feeling types tune more into the relationship itself and tend to notice detachment and criticism more quickly. What matters most to Feeling types is how much they care about something, how much they feel cared for, and harmony. Consistent with this, Muten (1991) suggested that in counseling, clients high on Agreeableness, the Big Five parallel of Feeling, are prone to feeling "silently wounded" (457) and to leaving counseling for this reason. This is *not* to say that Thinking types don't appreciate some warmth and acceptance but that they tend to need it less and as a preliminary or accompaniment to analysis rather than for its own sake.

Good communication is much more than knowing one's own type and matching modes (some of the time), but this knowledge does make good communication more likely, as the following example of an ENFP counselor and an ISFJ client, from Provost (1993), illustrates. The client was depressed. She saw herself as a slow learner, was impatient with complexity, and described her life as "dull and devoid of fun." Provost, an ENFP, controlled her natural, relatively bold approach: "Our relationship was a series of gentle pushes, cautious tries, and sometimes retreats" (52). She suspects that if she had tried to work at her own pace rather than her client's, the client would have clung to the familiar ways or left. Occasionally, Provost tried a paradoxical suggestion: "You're not ready to change—let's be more cautious." She also helped this client appreciate her (the client's) strengths, for example, organization (developed J) and warmth and caring (developed F), and they agreed on some specific goals, for example, to try out some additional learning strategies and to become more playful and flexible. Provost adds that she learned to be more patient from this client, and that "mutual respect and fascination with each other's processes were important elements in our counseling relationship" (52).

Examples of the main reactions and prejudices, according to MBTI theory, are that Introverts may feel overwhelmed, hurried, or invaded by Extraverts, and Es may see Is as dull and slow. Sensing types may be seen as boring by those with a preference for Intuition, and Ns as grandiose by Ss; Thinking types as obsessed with reasons and unsympathetic by Feeling types, and Fs as lacking any logic and too soft by Ts; Judging types as pushy and rigid by Perceiving types, and Ps as aimless and disorganized by Js. McCaulley (1996) saw the S–N difference as the most important, calling it a "chasm," and Pratt and Gray (1999) agreed: "differences in perception are the biggest source of conflict in the workplace" (227).

However, there are no rigorous empirical studies of these reactions as far as I know, and it would be interesting and useful to know how much of a problem they are and how people cope with them (assuming they are a problem). Jones and Sherman (1997) and Tieger and Barron-Tieger (2000) provide ideas and some relevant data on romantic relationships. A related question is how much type is related to willingness and ability to flex. Some types may be more likely to see matching or flexing as inauthentic, for example. Furthermore, we need to ask how helpful it is to know other persons' types as well as their current mode or language, and how effective in practice are the guidelines for improving communication suggested by Myers with Myers (1980, 209-210), Allen and Brock (2000), Dunning (2003), and others.

Overall, flexing and matching are tantalizing ideas implied by such metaphors as "in tune," "on the same wavelength," and "a meeting of minds" or, conversely, "no contact" and "speaking a different language." However, such metaphors point to rather than explain an experience, and the ideas remain intuitively compelling but vague. Moreover, there are hundreds of characteristics that could be central to a good match, for example attitudes, pace, sense of humor, multicultural factors, intellectual qualities, personality traits and types, values, interests—far too many characteristics and combinations to investigate them all. MBTI theory suggests some clear priorities.

THOMPSON'S APPROACH TO COMMUNICATION

I think Thompson's most stimulating suggestion about communication (following Yeakley) is that the language we generally use is determined by our extraverted function. Thus ENTJs and ISTJs tend to extravert and speak Thinking, ENFPs and INFPs Intuition, and so on (Thompson 1998a). In terms of type dynamics, extraverts mainly use the language of their dominant function when talking and introverts the language of their auxiliary function. Thompson (1998a) suggested four languages: S, N, T, and F. However, he has also developed a multilayered model, in which each type has a preferred language sequence; for example, ESTPs and ISTPs speak S most, T second most, F third, and N least. In addition to languages, there are dialects and styles, all neatly depicted in his Communication Wheel (Thompson 1998b). I find this too complicated to be useful, but experience and evidence may in time show that it is necessary.

Thompson (1998a) reported a .51 correlation between language spoken according to the theory and language actually spoken. Moreover, when a person did not speak the predicted first language, they nearly always spoke the predicted second one. Although these data are very promising for the main element (in my view) of his model, more details of method are required (numbers of participants of each type, how the observers were trained, etc.), and replication, to be convincing. Some of the cues used to assess language are listed in TABLE 8.1. Those marked with a (?) I find interesting but doubtful, but the others are consistent with MBTI theory. Are they enough to make accurate judgments of which language is being used?

It is also worth bearing in mind that Allen, and Brock and Allen (2000), find the four functional pairs (ST, SF, NT, NF) sufficient but that Thompson's model predicts problems with them. I don't know of any studies like Thompson's (1998a) that test how observable the languages are in Brock's sense. Allen and Brock include such characteristics as emphasizing:

- Practical, accurate facts and all the relevant tools (and "no fuzzy prelude"): ST
- Practical facts but more warmth and kindness: SF

TABLE 8.1

(S)	(N)
Present situation	*Possibilities*
Facts	*Big picture*
Practical	*Exaggerate*
Concrete	*Leaps*
Impatient (?)	*Bored by details*
Ramble (?)	*Read between the lines*
(T)	**(F)**
Businesslike	*Personal*
Serious	*Warm*
Impersonal	*Friendly*
Analytical	*Sensitive*
Intellectual	*Mood changes (?)*
Structured	*Take comments personally*

- To be treated as competent and intelligent by someone whom they see in the same way: NT

- To be treated as an individual: NF

The research methods on which these findings are based look sound, but there is not enough information in Allen and Brock (2000) to evaluate them properly.

Luzader (2001) suggested a further complication. On the basis of observing numerous communication labs, working mainly with professionals aged thirty to sixty years, she states that people consistently *talk* with the preference or mental function they use in the outside world and *write* with the preference they use inside. In addition, they *listen* with their auxiliary function.

To study talking, she asked type-alike groups to "select a topic they wanted to discuss and then to discuss it for 5 minutes" (38). She found that the topics selected and the "manner" in which the groups discussed them were "consistently type typical," but unfortunately no examples are given, and she is the only person whose observations are reported. Her key observation, which also supports an aspect of type dynamics, was that the group "rarely spoke with a mental function other than the one type theory predicts they would use with the outside world" (38). The combinations she observed were TJ, FJ, SP and NP and she comments that they "could easily be seen" (38). If verified, this is very important, partly because it is evidence for type dynamics, and partly for its implications for the Brock and Thompson models— although topic and context also influence which language is spoken.

To study writing, Luzader simply asked the group to write down the topics they wanted to discuss. She found that "As expected, they wrote with the function that type theory maintains they introvert" (38), and that introverts wrote more. Again, her results support type dynamics, and they provide an interesting twist on communication, but her ideas need and deserve a more rigorous test.

WRITING

Some people loathe writing, some avoid it, and some enjoy it. MBTI theory and research suggest several ways of increasing enjoyment and output—some of them exact opposites—that writers can try to find those that suit them best (DiTiberio and Jensen 1995; Jensen and DiTiberio 1989; Loomis 1999). Some of the strategies are missed or discounted in standard advice, but MBTI theory also implies that the standard strategies are ineffective for many people. This is useful in itself, but it goes much further to suggest that if you dislike writing, for example, this may be because you don't at the moment trust the natural writing style of your type. It therefore assumes that

- there is a different writing style which is most natural and most effective for each type
- knowing your type can help solve problems with writing
- people of all the psychological types can write effectively, and
- advice is likely to be biased by the psychological type of the person giving it. For example, setting up a timetable for writing seems more likely to be proposed by and to suit people with a preference for J.

The following general advice is based on studies of successful writers (Boice 1994), but each element may suit writers of some types more than others.

- Writing little and often is more pleasurable *and* more efficient than "binge-writing." He argued for "brief, daily sessions" of ten minutes to an hour.
- Take at least as long to take notes, organize them and play with them, as in writing, rewriting, and editing.

- When writing, make "tension checks" and relax if necessary.
- Aim for an average 1–2½ pages per hourly session.
- Write a draft and only later be concerned with writing it well.
- Rewrite several times.

An approach based on MBTI theory is to develop the strengths associated with your type first (TABLE 8.2), and add the opposite strengths later (TABLE 8.3, P. 104). It assumes that the opposite strengths should not be developed as much as the "true" strengths. This idea is applicable both to each piece of writing and to each person as a writer. MBTI theory assumes that good writing usually contains all or most of the elements listed, though with exceptions and varying emphases according to type and, of course, topic and genre. Type dynamics should play a central part.

Other aspects of writing well and comfortably may also be related to type, for example, fantasies and irrational beliefs about how success-ful writers write. Once exposed, the fantasies and beliefs can, of course, be challenged and replaced. Similarly, the conditions—physical and mental—in which people write best may be influenced by type. On the

TABLE 8.2

THE PREFERENCES AND WRITING: LIKELY STRENGTHS

Please consider which of the following are most true of you now or might come relatively easily to you.

E *Discussing the topic before writing. Fluency and breadth.*

I *Immersion in the topic, and depth.*

S *Details and concrete examples.*

N *Themes and variety of perspective.*

T *Objective style and criticism.*

F *Fluency.*

J *Focus, doing the writing, and stating conclusions.*

P *Breadth and revision.*

Table 8.3

The preferences and writing:
Adding the strengths of the opposite

Consider whether your writing would be improved by any of the following, or by more attention to them.

E *More structure and depth.*

I *Writing earlier.*

S *More themes and less detail.*

N *Examples. Fewer ideas.*

T *More "signposts," flow, and considering impact on others.*

F *More analysis and evidence.*

J *Revise a bit more and add some details.*

P *Add conclusions.*

other hand, some strategies may be generally helpful, though perhaps easier for some types than others. An example is free-writing, which was developed as a treatment for writer's block (Boice 1994) but can be used preventively too.

Giving Feedback in Interviewer Training

I will discuss two contexts for giving feedback: interviewer training and marking essays. However, the principles suggested may apply to coaching in work and sport, to verifying MBTI results, and to other forms of writing. Giving feedback is a high level multiple skill, requiring observation, empathy, and timing, as well as the more obvious skills of giving information: avoiding jargon, using short words and sentences, brevity, categorizing ("there are three things to remember here . . ."), variety of voice tone, and checking understanding (Ley 1988).

Heinrich and Pfeiffer (1989) developed a form for giving feedback to nursing and medical students on their interviewing. The form, a modified version of which is in TABLE 8.4, has not been evaluated as far as I know but is firmly based on MBTI theory. Thus, if the theory is valid, the method is likely also to be valid but still needs to be evaluated in its own right. How well does it counter the myth (quite prevalent) that there is one best way to interview or counsel, how well does it encourage trainees to focus on their strengths as well as areas to develop, and how effective is this compared to other approaches to interviewer and counselor training?

As in the approach to developing writing in tables 8.2 and 8.3, the main general principle in the form—though it may be useful to emphasize it more—is a Feeling one: to build on strengths by first confirming and developing your own type's strengths and then adding, to a lesser

TABLE 8.4

	THE PREFERENCES AND ASPECTS OF COUNSELING AND INTERVIEWING *(developed from Heinrich and Pfeiffer, 1989)*	
	Probable strengths	*Areas to work on?*
E	*Helping the client explore a wide range of issues* *Easy initial contact* *Thinking "on feet"*	*Paraphrasing more* *Using silence* *Helping client explore issues in sufficient depth* *Reaching the action stage too early*
I	*Helping the client explore a few issues in depth* *Reflecting on strategies, etc.* *Using silence*	*Paraphrasing more* *Helping the client move to action* *Helping client explore all relevant issues* *Ease of initial contact*
S	*Observing details* *Being realistic* *Helping client decide on practical action plans*	*Taking the overall picture into action* *Brainstorming (strategies, challenges, and actions)* *Using hunches*
N	*Seeing the overall picture* *Brainstorming* *Using hunches*	*Being specific* *Testing hunches* *Helping client decide on practical action plans*

(TABLE 8.4 *continued on next page*)

(TABLE 8.4 *continued from previous page*)

	Probable strengths	Areas to work on?
T	Being objective Challenging (i.e., from counselor's frame of reference)	Picking up emotions and feelings Being empathic (i.e., in client's frame of reference) Being warmer Challenging too early
F	Being warm Being empathic	Taking thoughts into account as well as emotions and feelings Coping with conflict and "negative" emotions Being more objective Challenging
J	Being organized	Being decisive Being flexible
P	Being spontaneous Being flexible	Being organized, e.g., keeping to time, structure of session

extent, the strengths of other types. For example, MBTI theory predicts that interviewers and counselors with a preference for Sensing will (a) tend to observe nonverbal communication well (better than Intuitive types) but tend to miss themes and neglect the general picture (unlike Ns). The suggested approach to giving feedback to people who prefer Sensing is to recognize their observation and other Sensing skills fully and, if these are indeed well developed, then to ask them to practice looking out for themes and other Intuitive skills.

Giving the feedback is of course an interaction, with the types of the person giving feedback and of the recipient playing a part. Type dynamics and attitude functions may also be relevant—in theory, should be relevant. For example, suppose the trainer is an ENTP and the trainee an ISFJ. The trainer can consider slowing his or her pace, giving the trainee more "space" for reflection, and using Sensing and Feeling skills for a while, as well as using their (the trainer's) probably more comfortable Intuitive (especially) and Thinking skills.

GIVING FEEDBACK ON ESSAYS

The influence of type on giving feedback on essays, and probably reports and other forms of writing, was illustrated well by Smith's (1993) study. She compared the comments on an essay of six lecturers with a preference for Thinking and six with a preference for Feeling, all of whom were experienced teachers of English and Introverted Intuitive types. All the lecturers put comments in the margins of the essay and summarized strengths and weaknesses (or "areas to develop") at the end. The Ts and the Fs all agreed on the mark for the essay, wrote about the same amount of feedback, and used similar numbers of questions and reactions, such as "You have two ideas here."

However, the differences were striking, especially as the department studied had agreed guidelines for giving feedback on essays. The F lecturers (five of whom were dominant Ns) praised the essay twice as much as the Ts and wrote twice as many suggestions. Smith (1993) suggests that this illustrates different philosophies of teaching. The Ts apparently believe that students do (or should) focus on weaknesses, on "what is the problem that needs solving?" (40); in other words, the emphasis is on what is wrong and how to fix it. Do T and F students share this view, and what is the impact of the different styles of feedback generally? Smith asked the lecturers about this and found greater concern in the F lecturers about students' feelings and greater emphasis in the Ts on content and potential learning.

The impact of feedback can be lifelong, so I think this is a key issue for research. Other questions to study include: What are the effects of the other preferences? How do students of different types react to the T and F styles of feedback? And when is each style the most effective?

Another idea about personality and feedback is that Extraverts respond more to reward and Introverts more to punishment. This has been supported quite strongly (Furnham and Heaven 1999, 201–5), but do Thinking and Feeling also play a part?

RECEIVING FEEDBACK

Type also seems very likely to be related to receiving feedback, another general and valuable skill. Thompson (1996b) suggested several ways of reacting to negative feedback, using an attitude-function framework, which is summarized here:

IS	*Tend to be calm outwardly and attack the next day. Need brief, specific feedback.*
ES	*Tend to respond immediately to feedback, to need recent, specific examples, and, like Es generally, want to discuss the feedback. They don't want to write an action plan.*
IN	*Tend to listen intently, and respond the next day. "The more visual the feedback, the better" (18).*
EN	*Tend to want the process to be flexible, fast moving and focused on ideas about how to improve.*
IT	*May become "philosophical or long-winded." Main response (critical) will come the next day.*
ET	*Tend to offer excuses and to challenge the feedback and the giver of feedback.*
IF	*May take days to recover.*
EF	*Tend to take the feedback personally and often make attacking comments.*

Jensen and DiTiberio (1989) made some related suggestions but used the preferences as a framework. These are consistent with Thompson about Extraverts and spoken feedback, Sensing types and concrete examples, and Intuitive types and possibilities. They add, however, that Feeling types tend to be more interested in comments on style and Thinking types in comments on content (in feedback on writing), and that Judging types are more interested in improving in the next essay (or report) and Perceiving types in improving the present one.

I think their ideas about "words of praise" are particularly worth investigating. Are the words (listed below) true, which other terms apply, and what role does type development play?

Linking this to Smith's (1993) study, discussed earlier, it seems likely that both lecturers and students have favorite terms of praise. MBTI

E	*Lively, vital*	I	*Thoughtful, depth*
S	*Careful, practical*	N	*Original, imaginative*
T	*Analytic, systematic*	F	*Enjoyable, heartfelt*
J	*Efficient, complete*	P	*Flexible, open-minded*

theory predicts what they are and their relative impact, and this seems to me another straightforward and potentially valuable area of research.

Empathy and Listening

Duan and Hill (1996) concluded their review of research on empathy with the quite damning comment that "the lack of specification and organization of different views of empathy has led to theoretical confusion, methodological difficulties, inconsistent findings and neglected areas of research" (269). MBTI theory offers a way of resolving some of the confusion because it predicts that different types will conceptualize and communicate empathy differently.

Churchill and Bayne (1998) tested this possibility with experienced counselors and found the following clear relationships between the preferences and conceptions and reported practice of empathy:

1) Counselors who preferred Sensing tended to refer to empathy as a state, and those who preferred Intuition tended to refer to it as a process.

2) Counselors who preferred Thinking and Judging had a more active conception and reported practice of empathy, while those who preferred Feeling and Perceiving referred to a passive approach.

A further predicted relationship, between preference for Thinking and cognitive empathy, and preference for Feeling and affective empathy, was close to statistical significance. This was perhaps the most obvious prediction from MBTI theory, and the failure to find strong support for it could be explained by the great emphasis on affect in most counselor training. I suspect that there is a real relationship, one more evident in counseling itself than in conceptions of counseling, but this belief needs to be tested.

Churchill and Bayne (2001) reported a qualitative analysis of the same interview data. They found, for example, that themes mentioned by those with a preference for Thinking indicate that they pay attention to many aspects of the situation—the language the client uses, nonverbal communication, trying to understand what meaning the story has for the client—and that they relate all these to theoretical concepts. These themes support the suggestion that Thinking types are more likely to emphasize the cognitive aspects of empathy and operate from their own frame of reference rather than that of the client (or perhaps just to be more analytic in their responses). In marked contrast, those with a preference for Feeling were more likely to emphasize "really listening," and "experiencing it with them." Those who reported that empathic communication comes easily to them were all Fs (five of eleven). None of these participants referred to "deeper levels of empathy," and their definitions of empathy included a reference to "being there" or "going by their own feelings," suggesting that for these counselors being empathic is something they take for granted.

A Case Study Example (from Churchill and Bayne 2001)
Two ISTJs contrasted with two INFPs

There were two female ISTJ counselors and two female INFP counselors amongst the participants. In response to the question: "When you're actually with a client, how do you come to understand what's going on for your client?" one ISTJ replied:

> "I take very little notice of the referral letter. I ask what's bothering the client. I listen and try to see what could be different, are they looking at things . . . might they be blinkered? *What* are the issues likely to be? How receptive are they to me? I look for tension—that's usually reliable, the relevance of tensions to what they're recounting and where they are, and their resistances."

The other said:

> "Well, first, what is the problem? I would ask for expansion and clarification—what's the cognition behind the problem? I look for patterns of behavior, their emotional level because silly things can go out of proportion, *I look at their cognitions, and distortions in their cognitions, reading meanings into things which are not there.* I'm actively gathering information. I try to get into their core belief system: what does it mean to them? Where do their core beliefs come from: parents, their peer group?"

The sections in italics show a similar concern to identify how the client's perceptions might be idiosyncratic.

The INFPs replied very differently. One said:

> "Well, the obvious things: if I've had a similar experience I can empathise. I try to enter into the situation, imagine what it

must be like in my head; sometimes it moves me to tears; understanding; I imagine myself in it and what it must be like."

The other said:

"Primarily through listening. Listen listen listen listen, to the story and the underneath, and to the feelings, which are then checked out, with the client, as tentatively as I can unless I'm really sure. A lot of reflection, I do a lot of empathy. At the beginning of a process, you know, if it's a client I'm seeing for the first time or haven't seen very often, that's basically all I do, and some questions as open as they can be. I'm using less and less questions, actually, I have to say. With people that I've been working with for some time, I use a lot of immediacy, in that I know that that is my own particular style and that has evolved, and I think immediacy is a very powerful tool, and it brings into play the mutuality that Rogers talks about in the process."

The contrast between the two pairs is thus very marked: in particular, the ISTJs emphasize cognitions, and the INFPs emotions. Another dramatic contrast is the way the INFP counselors use their own emotional responses. For the ISTJs there is a drive to plan the therapy, define the problems, identify goals; for the INFPs it seems more important to fully enter the client's world. Their different theoretical orientations (the ISTJs were respectively cognitive and psychodynamic; the INFPs person-centered, and integrative on a psychodynamic foundation) seem to matter less than their psychological types.

Research like this can help practicing counselors develop greater awareness of their own strengths and weaknesses in being empathic. Similarly, counselor trainers may tend to emphasize those aspects of empathy that are most consistent with their own personality and neglect other aspects. Acknowledging the multifaceted nature of empathy will help those of their students who are of very different types understand how they can develop empathic qualities and skills, and make assessing them fairer.

The Churchill and Bayne (1998, 2001) study has several limitations. The sample was a small one, though the participants were all experienced counselors, giving greater validity than a larger sample of counseling students. A greater problem with the sample is its cultural homogeneity: only one participant was Asian, the others white. Other limitations are the unknown relationship between participants' conceptions of empathy and their behavior, and the weaknesses of the qualitative approach adopted. Future studies might most usefully focus on replication, on counselors of psychological types underrepresented in the study, and on using a variety of interviewers. For example, the interviewer/interpreter in this study was female, white, middle-class, trained in person-centered counseling but integrative (mainly cognitive and humanistic) in approach, and an ENTP.

This exploratory study shows quite clearly the multifaceted nature of empathy and that, as predicted by MBTI theory, different psychological types tend to emphasize some facets while paying less or no attention to those emphasized by others.

AN EXERCISE ON EMPATHY AND LISTENING

As far as possible, form function-attitude groups and type or temperament groups and ask them to discuss "When you're listening really well, what exactly are you doing?"

Good outcome. Profound differences can appear as in the Churchill and Bayne (1998, 2001) research. For example, Introverted Feeling groups report comparing their own previous experience with the client's experience. The obvious risks are of confusing the two and in particular attributing their own emotions to the client, and being wrong. Extraverted Feeling groups report focusing on their clients' emotions directly, putting themselves aside. An Intuitive Thinking group reports that listening to what is actually said is a struggle and one they often give up. Rather, they are aware of lots of thinking, complexity, and assumptions.

The main possibilities for emphasis in listening may be the following:

- What is actually said, with little or no interpretation, inwardly or outwardly (related, in theory, to S)
- Connections (N)
- Implications, analysis, theories (T, especially NT)
- Emotions, values (F)
- Action, problem solving (J and SP)

Luzader (2001) studied listening—paraphrasing—with groups of people who were familiar with MBTI theory and knew their types, but who presumably weren't trained to listen. She observed that paraphrasing (after two minutes of a partner talking) is done with the auxiliary function—not an obvious prediction from MBTI theory, even though it was her hypothesis—and that Extraverts usually paused and Introverts rarely did, when the opposite behaviors are usually characteristic. On the other hand, she observed the Introverts being more still and quiet during the two minutes.

I discussed Luzader's approach to talking and writing earlier in this chapter, and I think the same general conclusions apply to her work on listening: these are creative and stimulating ideas and findings that deserve more rigorous testing.

CONCLUSIONS

Communication is one of the main areas of MBTI application. A useful start has been made on clarifying and testing its assumptions and ideas. I discussed and compared the general approaches of Brock and Thompson and specific applications of MBTI theory to writing, feedback, and empathy and listening, and gave examples of the various kinds of research that have begun to clarify and refine them.

Chapter 9

HOW CAN TYPE BE OBSERVED MORE ACCURATELY?

F or many applications of Myers Briggs Type Indicator® (MBTI®) theory, it is helpful to be able to make accurate judgments of other people's psychological types. Two exceptions occur: when the practitioner includes a sufficient range of choices to suit all the types, for example, in a workshop, a classroom, or an advertising campaign (though I expect most campaigns need to be targeted more at some types than others), and when mode or "language" is judged. The language used—discussed in chapter 8—is more variable than type and may be easier to observe accurately.

However, observing type accurately is obviously desirable for understanding oneself, friends, partners, relatives, colleagues, and others, and often MBTI results, let alone verified results, are not available. Fortunately, it seems that most people, much of the time, make reasonably accurate judgments of personality (Bayne 1995; Binning et al. 1999; Funder 1995, 1999). Moreover, accurate judgments can sometimes be made on very limited information—a few seconds interaction with complete strangers—and are made in spite of the numerous factors that can interfere with them. Nevertheless, because some judgments are wrong, and because errors can have such a great impact, it is worth trying to improve one's accuracy.

In this chapter, I consider obstacles to accuracy, discuss strategies for improving accuracy, and critically evaluate four frameworks: those of Niednagel, Delunas, Tieger and Barron-Tieger, and Rutledge. Obstacles and strategies were discussed in Bayne (1995) and are summarized with some refinements and additions in the next two sections.

OBSTACLES TO ACCURACY

MBTI theory suggests four obstacles to observing type accurately. First is the fact that preferences cannot be observed directly but only through clues in behavior. Second, some preferences are more visible than others. According to type dynamics, it should be particularly difficult to observe the preferences used in an introverted way (the dominant function for Introverts, the auxiliary for Extraverts). Moreover, the perceiving functions, Sensing and Intuition, may be more difficult to observe accurately simply because the process of taking in information is less visible than the making of decisions. People are also more likely to explain their decisions to others than how they take in information, although this does happen: "I'm very realistic," "Give me the facts," or "I'm an ideas person."

A third obstacle is type development. As people learn to use their opposite functions better, the observer may be seeing evidence of these developed functions rather than a person's preferences. Fourth, there are other situations in which people may exhibit false clues, which only a skilled and knowledgeable observer would detect as invalid. These include people who are under stress or who are making a special effort over a short period of time to perform, for example, in a selection interview, with a boss, or on a date.

Moreover, many people in each of these situations behave *authentically,* which complicates accurate observations even more. For example, Fletcher (1981) studied beliefs and self-presentation strategies in selection interviews and found that 71 percent of his student sample agreed with the statement that "they had to be completely honest with the interviewer." They differed more on whether or not "One should try to project a particular 'image' of the sort of person you would like the interviewer to think you actually are" (36 percent agreed; 23 percent were uncertain; and 41 percent disagreed). Overall, an honest and cooperative approach in beliefs and strategies was favored, though with marked individual differences. MBTI theory would predict NFs to be the most honest (or naive, from another point of view), but how confusing it is for interviewers if some candidates believe in directness and honesty, some that the best strategy is to be "economical with the truth," and some that lies are justified, and they all behave accordingly. The general point here is that the ability to fake (lying, diplomacy, self-deception) is a central characteristic of human beings, and one that no good theory of personality could leave out.

The effects of social, cultural, and historical contexts on MBTI results and falsification were discussed by Robinson (2001), in particular Battle's finding that U.S. black respondents are more likely than whites to misreport themselves as STJs. The MBTI questionnaire does try to measure "being" but hasn't succeeded with some members of this group: they present their "doing" rather than their "being" selves. Robinson argues that "falsifying" is "a dangerous and inaccurate term" (200) for this choice—dangerous because it may turn African Americans away from MBTI theory and applications because they may believe it is "yet another tool used by the establishment to demean the group," inaccurate because it doesn't describe major aspects of their behavior: their adaptation to oppression, their "putting on a face." I think the key issues here are how widespread the effect is, and, of course, how to counter it. In addition, whether the term *type falsification* is dangerous or insulting or not in this situation, MBTI theory is clear about the negative effects of behaving in ways that are significantly inconsistent with type: frustration, exhaustion, and so on. Is the prediction accurate for this group?

Here are other general obstacles and factors in accurate observations:

- We look initially for meaning, then fail to notice alternative evidence.
- We give disproportionate power to our first impressions.
- We assume that if a person is like us in one way, he or she is like us in other ways too.
- We use stereotypes.
- We use a few favorite concepts.
- We underestimate the effect of the situation on the behavior of the person observed.
- Some people have more visible personalities and behave more consistently than others.
- The characteristic being observed, Extraversion, for example, is generally more observable.
- The situation and whether it allows people to express themselves in a genuine way.
- The number of people observing. Three or four observers seem to be optimum. More observers give diminishing returns.

- The number of observations. If three observations are made at different times or in different kinds of situations, accuracy increases.

- How well the observer knows the person observed. Even preferences that are generally easier to observe, like Extraversion and Introversion, are observed more accurately by friends and spouses than by new acquaintances.

General Strategies for Improving Accuracy

It is easy and tempting to make quick judgments of a person's psychological type, including one's own, and mistakes are easily made, however striking or compelling the evidence appears to be. The ideal evidence for accurate judgment of any personality characteristic is a broad, representative sample of behavior gathered by a skillful observer over a long period and in a variety of situations. Personality questionnaires and interviews seek, of course, to be a shortcut. In practice, accurate judgments can be made without the ideal conditions because MBTI and Big Five theory and research suggest that people do generally behave in tune with their types. However, the judgments should still be made tentatively and with care. The following strategies, based on Kenrick and Funder (1988) and others, all seek to slow down our normal processes in the interests of increasing accuracy.

- Look for patterns over time and across situations.
- To test for consistency, deliberately observe the person at different times and in different situations.
- Treat first impressions as hypotheses.
- Then concentrate on both confirming and disproving those hypotheses through additional observation, looking for evidence *against* first impressions too.
- Look for alternative interpretations of the evidence. Particularly watch for the effects of the situation. Some situations such as interviews and first dates tend to skew behavior much more than others. Also consider whether stress, eagerness to please, or cultural or organizational norms are affecting behavior in this observation.
- Recognize the ambiguity of behavior. Look at the motive for behaving in this way as well as the

behavior itself. Consider asking why the person behaves as they do or, more subtly, ask and observe what energizes them and what tires them most and most quickly. Observe how they do things too.

- Become aware of your own stereotypes and favorite criteria and allow for them.

  Try jotting down your impressions of, say, ten people, or look at some references you've already written and see if there are qualities or criteria that you repeat. You may tend to look for these at the expense of other qualities.

- Compare observations with other people.

  Even a person who is not knowledgeable about type can confirm or deny what you think you are observing.

- Deepen your knowledge of type theory.

  For example, SPs can be mistaken for Js because of their quick decisions, but notice their flexibility; IFs can seem like Es because of their interest in people, but notice their greater need for time alone. Then there are type dynamics, type development, and other factors to take into account.

- Use a framework or system.

  Several systems for observing the preferences and therefore types accurately have been developed. I will outline and evaluate four systems or frameworks, those of Niednagel (1997), Delunas (1992), Tieger and Barron-Tieger (1998), and Rutledge (1999).

Niednagel

Niednagel (1997) claims that MBTI results are much less accurate than his own judgments. His view is that the MBTI is wrong about *half* the time and that he is generally right. Indeed, he uses the term "Brain Types"® to emphasize this point. Brain Types are the sixteen psychological types of MBTI theory, but as assessed by his method. His method can be very quick: he writes that after watching "a minute or two of highlights on each player" of a basketball team, he could inform them of each player's respective Brain Type, with corresponding strengths and weaknesses (23). However, his standard method is careful observation of conversations, behavior, attitudes, and movements, including "thoughts, syntax, diction, voice inflection, and so forth" (48). His fee in the year 2000 for assessing Brain Type was 300 dollars (web site:

www.braintypes.com)—very reasonable if his method is indeed as precise and the MBTI questionnaire as invalid as he claims.

Take two specific, and to me, thought-provoking but dubious, illustrations of his general position first:

> Many who rely on the popular psychological types approach, and do not understand Brain Types, believe ISTJs are one of the most commonly found types in America. They are greatly misled. Men in particular score their quizzes as ISTJs—placing high value on the reserved, pragmatic, logical, and organized traits of the "Investigator." Utilizing Brain Types®, especially its motor skill traits, quickly reveals the true ISTJ. In reality, the "Investigator" is one of the least found Types in the US. (302)

And:

> I have even come to realize that some of the most well-known, highly educated leaders in typology circles have typed themselves incorrectly. (383)

His general argument is that, when answering psychometric questionnaires, people "often try to portray how they want to be seen instead of how they really are," misunderstand the questions, read too much into them, answer them too quickly, or are significantly affected by mood or situation (383). These are standard problems with all personality questionnaires, and I believe that the MBTI questionnaire is more robust and valid than Niednagel does and that the evidence on its validity supports my view.

However, the main point here is that Niednagel claims 100 percent accuracy for his own system, if it is carefully applied (384). More specifically, he claims that his own observational skills and judgment are extremely accurate. The problems are: (1) How does he know? (Because people agree with him. But how do *they* know? People agree with astrologers and tea-leaf readers too). (2) That he is the person judging both elements—Brain Type and skill at sport—so he can alter one or the other to fit his theory. Suppose he sees someone playing tennis well, then he may be more likely to assess that person as, say, ISTP for that reason. The approach is therefore in serious danger of being circular, self-fulfilling, and self-deceiving. More objective measures are needed.

Delunas

Delunas (1992) writes that she rarely uses personality tests in her clinical practice but relies on observation: "this is not difficult when one knows what clues to look for in adults and children" (46). Her guidelines are structured around questions that the observer asks him- or herself, not the person observed.

Q.1. Does this person seem to be more *abstract* or more *concrete* in his or her orientation toward the world?

The clues that Delunas recommended include more interest in facts or in ideas, choice of reading, more interest in what (of people or things) than why, and more interest in what is practical or in what is possible.

Q.2. Does this person seem to be more *cooperative* or more *pragmatic* in his or her approach to doing things?

Here Delunas is using temperament theory, which sees SJs and NFs as cooperative, and SPs and NTs as pragmatic. On this view, SJs and NFs tend to ask "Is it right?" (legal, ethical), SPs and NTs, "Is it useful?"

Delunas doesn't suggest more specific clues for this assessment, but Keirsey does (see next chapter). The next step for Delunas is to tentatively place the observed person in one of the four temperament groups (49):

Concrete + pragmatic = SP

Concrete + cooperative = SJ

Abstract + pragmatic = NT

Abstract + cooperative = NF

She then crosschecks by taking the basic needs of each temperament into account and considering whether or not the observed person's values (inferred from their behavior) fit their provisional temperament. In particular, she observes (a) what the person likes to do and (b) what he or she likes most about doing it, and looks for patterns. For example, she reports that many of her SP clients are in jobs they find boring, but asked what they really enjoy (and have enjoyed) they describe "exciting, hands-on, action-oriented activities, often involving risk" (50).

Another crosscheck is to ask how the person deals with rules. She suggests that SJs *follow* rules, and expect others to do the same; NFs *bend* rules, especially to help others; NTs *question* all rules and disregard those they see as foolish or illogical; SPs are likely to *break* rules. She quotes an SP as explaining, "I'd rather ask for forgiveness than ask for permission!"

At this point in Delunas's system, temperament has been assessed and crosschecked. Her next step is to focus on Judging–Perceiving for two of the temperaments (SP and SJ) through the question: "Is this person more of a *director* or more of an *informant?*"

Directing is telling or suggesting to people what to do. Informing is giving information and options rather than suggesting a choice or making a decision. Directing is saying, "Lets go to see X." Informing is saying "Well, there's X, which the reviewers say is exciting, and Y, which has Juliette Binoche in it."

She also suggests at this stage, for SPs and SJs, looking for evidence of impersonal and objective (T) versus personal and subjective (F).

To observe J-P in the other two temperaments (NT and NF) she asks the director/informant question and (my terms) whether they tend to focus on one thing at a time (J) or multi-task (P), and whether they tend to be more structured (J) or more flexible (P).

Finally, Extraversion–Introversion is assessed through asking about comfort in talking to strangers, and being energized more through interacting with others (E) or through time alone (I). Overall, Delunas's approach seems to me to have some promising elements but perhaps to be unnecessarily complicated.

Tieger and Barron-Tieger

The third system I consider here is Tieger and Barron-Tieger's (1998). It is written in their usual extremely clear, practical, and upbeat style, though to call their approach "scientifically validated" (4), "of enormous benefit to anyone who enjoys dealing with others or who needs to" (5), and one that will "help you instantly identify the preferred communication style of each customer" (5), is in my view rather too upbeat. Similarly, they probably overstate the strength of the clues to the preferences when they write: "For example, there are numerous behaviors that Sensors are much more likely to engage in than Intuitives" (63). "Much" is too strong in my reading of the research literature. However, they do add a realistic word of caution about looking for patterns and combinations of factors, and that some of the clues are subtle.

Overall, their approach is to discuss clues for each of the preferences, such as the energy of Extraverts—lots of hand movements, wider range of facial expressions—and the quieter, calmer air of Introverts. And here I find them very thoughtful and stimulating, though again overstated. For example, they say that Is seem to communicate the message, "what's your hurry? ...We've got plenty of time." Well, not ISTJs in my experience. On the other hand, they do describe the clues in a deliberately dramatic way for clarity, and it is tedious to keep writing "tend" and "some."

They are dubious about occupational choice as a clue, stating that "most people have jobs that do not make use of their natural talents" (66). I welcome the implication of this for observing type accurately: that how people choose their work, what they like and don't like about it, and fantasy jobs may be more useful clues than the occupation itself. But I'd like to know their evidence for a widespread lack of fit between natural talents and occupation, and therefore low job satisfaction. The general view in the literature on job satisfaction seems to be more positive (Bayne, 2004).

The clues for the preferences and the temperaments are organized under a variety of headings, including appearance, demeanor, language, body language, occupation, communication style, and interests. They also analyze and suggest clues for more complex aspects of type such as the influence of gender on Extraverted Feeling. For example, "In contrast to people who Extravert Feeling and who often have sparkly eyes, FPs and TJs often have what can best be described as sad eyes" (115). My reaction is to be intrigued and to wonder, Is this really true? Is there good research on observing sparkly and sad eyes (and seeing if they are related to type)? Most of the clues they suggest follow directly from MBTI theory, but some are questionable, for example, making lists as a clue for J. I think most people make lists and that what varies is their attitude toward their lists.

Tieger and Barron-Tieger suggest three variations of their system:

- Preference clues first, then temperament and the E–I Feeling pattern as checks
- Temperament and E–I Feeling pattern, then E–I
- E–I Feeling pattern first, then temperament and preferences

Each of these variations may be the best in a particular situation (124). Choosing which to use is left open to the observer without guidelines. Is one more generally useful? Can the system be simpler and still be effective?

Rutledge
Rutledge (1999) suggested a "logical three step process" for observing type in an ethical way:

Step one: Temperament

Step two: Moving beyond temperament

Step three: Beware!

Step one involves looking for patterns of behavior in a number of situations and focusing on the four temperaments because their patterns are "so distinct" and their predictive powers "so great" (192). Rutledge notes that other elements of temperament theory are also useful for type watching: the "drivers," limitations, leadership and communication styles. So far his general approach is the same as Delunas's, but his method is less structured.

Rutledge's second stage is also similar to Delunas's. If you think someone's behavior suggests he or she is an NF or NT, the next step is to look for J versus P, and then E versus I. If you think the person is an SP, the next step is E–I, then T–F. If you think the person is an SJ, it's T–F, then E–I. The suggested behaviors (clues) to watch for are consistent with MBTI theory and with those discussed in the next chapter. With the SPs and SJs, Rutledge is leaving the introverted function (according to type dynamics) to last, which is the beginning of a rationale for his framework and seems to me neat but unnecessary.

Stage three offers some caveats. The first bears repeating: "Good typewatching looks for patterns of behavior over time and preferably in numerous settings" (199). On the other hand, Brock's and Thompson's approaches to communication both imply that this may be unnecessarily cautious.

Second, he suggests, as did Brownsword (1987), that SJs and NFs both like to belong to institutions (though for different motives) and SPs and NTs both like to act autonomously (again for different motives), and that this can be misleading. I think this is another example of an obstacle, and that it may be no more important than other obstacles. The third caveat is that the most important evidence comes from the individual's input and verification, though the context would play a part here. Overall, this seems a relatively straightforward approach, consistent with MBTI theory.

CONCLUSIONS

The key general issue for observing type accurately is which system is most effective when MBTI results—verified or not—are not available.

Overall, I think Niednagel's approach depends too much on a specialized set of skills and lacks good evidence. Moreover, if this evidence were to be gathered, it would mean a radical rethink of the MBTI literature. Delunas's approach has some promising elements but may be unnecessarily complicated. Tieger and Barron-Tieger and Rutledge are clearer and provide relatively straightforward frameworks for other approaches or elements of them. However, some of the clues they suggest are arguable, and their methods need to be evaluated. Finally, and quite differently, it might be very interesting to investigate psychological type and the strategies used by good judges (if they exist): Does their type affect their strategy? Do different types use very different strategies? Are some types better judges or is type development the most influential factor?

Chapter 10

CLUES FOR OBSERVING THE
PREFERENCES AND TEMPERAMENTS

n his 2001 review of personality theory and research, Funder makes the important point that we know very little about which behaviors are related to personality characteristics: "the catalog of basic facts concerning the relationships between personality and behavior remains thin. If, for example, one were to go to the literature and look for a list of contextualised behaviors that had been shown to be robustly associated with, say, extraversion, one would find surprisingly little" (211). Funder adds that "as for what extraverts have been observed to actually do, beyond some indication that they speak loudly (Scherer 1979), little would be found. Even less information is available about the behavioral correlates of other personality traits" (211).

There is some good research on specific behavior related to the Big Five and to the preferences, but, as Funder states and perhaps because this kind of research lacks glamour, not much of it. I discuss some examples in this chapter, focusing first on the preferences, then on the temperaments, and briefly on whole types. An important practical finding is that single clues seem rarely to be enough: accuracy is much more likely if the observer is patient and open-minded and looks for patterns or themes. If one or two clues were generally enough, there would be no need for the Myers Briggs Type Indicator® (MBTI®) questionnaire.

THE PREFERENCES

Extraversion versus Introversion may be the most visible preference. A clear finding is that Es tend to speak more loudly, more quickly, and with fewer pauses (Scherer 1979; Funder and Sneed 1993). They also tend to speak in a more cheerful, enthusiastic, and expansive way and pay more compliments (Thorne 1987). Thorne's study is particularly good evidence for E-I differences and also for their effects on others. For example, she found that Es' conversations with other Es were the most expansive and that Is found conversations with Es easier and more refreshing (generally, of course, and, I suspect, for a short time only!). Similar studies of the other preferences would be of great value.

A more speculative E-I clue is that Es overstate and tend to repeat themselves (Kroeger and Thuesen 1988, 65). Kroeger and Thuesen further suggest that Es gesture more and are more facially expressive. To some extent this is part of defining E-I—a concrete version of "outgoing" versus "reserved"—and Funder and Sneed (1993) found that Es do indeed tend to be more expressive in face, voice, and gestures. It is worth including details of Funder and Sneed's methodology, partly to show their thoroughness but also to allow critical thinking about this kind of research.

Funder and Sneed videotaped opposite-sex pairs who did not know each other talking for 5 minutes about whatever they liked. A few weeks later, each person was videoed again with another partner they did not know. The way each of the 140 participants behaved was then categorized, using sixty-two statements describing a fairly general level of behavior, for example, "behaved in a cheerful manner." The statements also described Big Five characteristics. The categorizers were carefully trained, and on average six of them judged each tape.

Each of the participants was also asked for the names of two people whom they knew well, and these people described the participant's personality, choosing from the set of 62 Big Five statements. They then watched a tape of someone they didn't know and used the same set of statements to describe the personality of this person. Finally, a separate group rated the sets of statements on how likely they were to be valid cues in the particular setting (i.e., a five-minute videotaped conversation between strangers). Here the researchers were studying beliefs or implicit personality theories.

In summary, the researchers had three sets of data for each participant:

1) Their behavior in two brief one-to-one conversations with different strangers

2) A description of their personality, in terms of five factor theory, by people who knew them well

3) Judgments of their personality, in terms of five factor theory, by categorizers who did not know them

Taking only the cues with the largest correlations, of .25 and above, the most valid cues for each preference, in the sense that observations from the tape and observations by people who know the person well in everyday life agreed with each other, were as follows:

Extraversion	*Is expressive in face, voice, or gestures* *Has high enthusiasm* *Speaks in a loud voice* *Exhibits social skills* *Is talkative*
Introversion	*Expresses insecurity or sensitivity* *Has awkward interpersonal style* *Behaves in fearful or timid manner* *Is reserved and unexpressive* *Keeps partner at a distance* *Shows lack of interest in interaction*

In this research, Extraversion and Introversion were among the most visible personality characteristics. There also seems to be a bias against Introversion in the language used.

Sensing and Intuition (called Openness in five factor theory) were much less visible in this study; there were no cues at the .25 level or above. For Thinking and Feeling there were the following:

Thinking	*Acts irritable* *Talks at, not with, partner* *Expresses skepticism or cynicism*
Feeling	*Behaves in a cheerful manner* *Laughs frequently*

Like the standard five factor descriptions, these terms are less glowing than those in typical MBTI descriptions. They are, however, consistent with them and, by definition, observable and valid clues for T and F. Surprisingly, J and P were also less visible in this research and the cues seemed to overlap those for the other factors. One level of MBTI theory implies that, because they are ways of gathering information and therefore internal processes, S and N are harder to observe accurately than E–I and J–P. The research so far on the related Big Five characteristic of Openness suggests few valid cues, supporting the "less visible" viewpoint. However, other levels of MBTI theory—the function-pairs and the temperaments—contradict it, and other research has found useful clues for S–N and J–P (e.g., Thorne and Gough 1991, summarized and discussed in Bayne 1995).

An example of a clue which has been suggested for S–N is that Ss tend to "take things literally" (Kroeger and Thuesen 1988, 68). Kroeger and Thuesen suggest asking 'How was your day?' because Ss will tend to give a step-by-step account, Ns an overview. Other factors, like tiredness, the current state of your relationship with the speaker, and E–I, will have an effect. Another way of expressing and refining this S characteristic is to say that Ss tend to be more interested than Ns in either what is actually happening (SPs more) or what has happened (SJs).

For Kroeger and Thuesen, T–F is "the most difficult process to discern" (1988, 70). Research on the related Big Five factor does not support their view (Funder and Sneed 1993). An example of a clue for T–F is that Fs are more concerned to please others, and need harmony more. This characteristic of Fs also explains the link between F and emotions—a source of confusion in type theory. Fs necessarily take more interest in emotions in contrast to Ts' greater focus on reasons. Both Ts and Fs have emotions, "but Feelers prefer to experience them while Thinkers prefer to understand them" (Kroeger and Thuesen 1988, 71).

The clue of needing to please others has not been tested empirically and as a characteristic would be influenced by other factors, like self-esteem, anxiety, beliefs, and specific situations. Consistent with it, Fs have been found to have softer, friendlier expressions and readier smiles, to behave more cheerfully, and to laugh more frequently than Ts (Funder and Sneed 1993).

A more concrete possible clue is that a preference for T may be associated with greater use of words like "think" and "analyze," and a preference for F with greater use of "feel," "love," and other emotion words (Seegmiller and Epperson 1987). This finding may be worth replicating and extending (Bayne 1995, 104). However, relationships between language and personality tend to be complex and slight, at least so far (Pennebaker and King 1999; Pennebaker and Lay 2002). Pennebaker and Lay see research in the area as at an early stage and find that "it is not yet clear what features of language are the best or most reliable markers of situational influences and personality style" (280).

Studies of the relationship between expressive or nonverbal behavior and personality have a long history in psychology (DePaulo 1993) and it is widely accepted in everyday life that there is a relationship, as illustrated by such plausible activities as graphology (Bayne and O'Neill 1988). DePaulo discusses some of the complexities of carrying out research in this area, emphasizing an impression management perspective.

Research on clues for J–P and the related Big Five characteristic of Conscientiousness has not so far supported a common view in the MBTI literature (e.g., Kroeger and Thuesen 1988, 66; Murray 1995) that J–P is "perhaps the easiest preference to spot." Funder and Sneed (1993) found much stronger clues for the factors related to E–I and T–F. However, there was clear support for Js tending to be more orderly and neat than Ps in Ware and Rytting (1989). They took photographs of the insides of cars and found that Js' cars tended, quite strongly, to be more orderly and with fewer objects than the cars of Ps. On the other hand, Kroeger and Thuesen suggest—subtly (and accurately?)—that "Perceivers, because of their adaptive, flexible nature, are capable of appearing like Judgers—though Judgers are less able to exist within the flexible world of Perceivers" (67), which is the kind of complicating factor discussed earlier.

Funder and Sneed also investigated popular but possibly invalid cues—those actually used by observers. These largely agreed with the valid cues. Taking a higher base of .3, the cues listed earlier were used to judge E and I, plus "initiates humor" and "dominates the interaction." "Expresses interest in fantasy and daydreams" was used to identify N; "expresses warmth" plus the two cues that are included, were used for F; and "interrupts partner" for T. "Displays ambition," "shows genuine interest in intellectual matters," "exhibits high degree of intelligence," were the cues (valid or not!) used for J; and there were none at .3 or above for P. Overall, these data support the view that people tend to use the cues they think they use, and use valid cues the most when judging Extraversion (E–I) and Agreeableness (T–F).

Are the most accurate judgments based on the careful weighting of numerous low-validity cues or best achieved through *overall impressions?* Although overall impressions are vaguer and fuzzier, they were found to be generally more useful than *very* specific behaviors by Ambady and Rosenthal (1993, 439). They give the example of a smile, which can be interpreted as positive (genuinely warm) or negative (threatening) depending on accompanying behavior and context, but, of course, a smile of a particular kind is still a fairly specific observation to make.

A huge number of clues have been suggested in the MBTI literature, some specifically with the aim of making accurate judgments (e.g., Tieger and Barron-Tieger 1998; Allen and Brock 2000), others as part of basic descriptions. I think they need to be reviewed and evaluated and tested further.

A different approach to clues for type is to take an area of behavior, observe it, and speculate about it. Two examples are discussed next: money and leisure.

An Alternative Approach to Clues: Two Examples

Money and Shopping

How people spend money (or don't spend it) seems likely to be a useful clue to their type. Indeed, Linder (2000a) believes that dominant function is the most influential factor; if he's right, then a central part of type dynamics is supported too. Linder suggests the following relationships, based on his work as a financial adviser. Most are consistent with basic type theory but are an interesting and potentially useful elaboration of it, both for general theory and specific application. His suggestions are shown in TABLE 10.1.

Linder (2000b) suggests that temperament (in Keirsey's sense) reveals motivations about money, and of course vice versa. Thus, SPs spend to feel free and excited; SJs are careful and use money to achieve security and stability; NTs try to spend it perfectly (demonstrating competence); and NFs tend to ignore it. He has also found that early life experience can complicate the relationship between temperament and

TABLE 10.1

IS	*Plan and save. Strong loyalty to stores and brands.*
ES	*Saving is impractical. Buy it now.*
IN	*Spend elegantly and tastefully. "The ideal is more important than the cost." "Insightful gift givers."*
EN	*"Natural savers." Linder's rationale is that ENTPs and ENFPs save for future possibilities.*
IT	*"Highly analytical comparison shoppers" who are concerned with the intrinsic value—the right price—of something.*
ET	*The most organized approach: records, receipts, etc.*
IF	*"Of all types, money matters least."*
EF	*Use money to care for others.*

money, for example an NF trying to behave like her NT mother. While this is a realistic complication, it does, of course, reduce the value of behavior with money as a clue if it is at all widespread.

Linder's general approach to giving financial advice is to affirm that each temperament or type's approach is OK, and to make suggestions for improvement if the person wishes. For example, NTs can analyze too much, both for themselves and those they talk to. Each type might also, without discarding their strengths and adopting an approach that doesn't suit them, see if any aspects of other approaches seem worth trying.

Leisure

Choice of leisure appears to be another particularly good source of clues for type. However, other factors, like social class, are strongly involved (Argyle 1996), and the same hobby may fulfill various motives. In addition, it may not be so much the hobby as the person's style of doing it that is the useful clue. Again, careful and sensitive observation is needed. A further reason for studying leisure is that some less obvious predictions have been made which, if supported, would enrich MBTI theory. For example, why (if they do) do ESTJs tend to have stronger links with animals than most types? Provost (1990) is the author who has written most about type and leisure and her ideas are summarized in TABLE 10.2.

OPP, in a 2001 newsletter, suggested MBTI vacations (TABLE 10.3), which worked well in an informal survey (I read the list and

TABLE 10.2

ISTJ *Tend to be serious and thorough. Computer games, Trivial Pursuit, golf, chess.*	**ISFJ** *Planned activities with close friends or relatives, e.g., eating. Nature, TV.*
ISTP *Mechanical things. Shooting, scuba diving, stand-up comedy, tricks.*	**ISFP** *Quiet, friendly. Crafts, art.*
ESTP *Tend to be very active and competitive. Racing, boxing.*	**ESFP** *Tend to be very social, warm, friendly.*
ESTJ *Tend to organize and run things. Community organizations and using their interest in nature.*	**ESFJ** *Tend to be warm-hearted and enjoy planning parties and less competitive sports.*
INFJ *Tend to like reflective, solitary activities, e.g., music, reading, collecting.*	**INTJ** *Tend to be critical and serious. Games of strategy, museums, study.*
INFP *Private enthusiasms. Writing, photography, films, books. Nature.*	**INTP** *Tend to be solitary. Reading, chess.*
ENFP *Tend to be warmly enthusiastic about many kinds of leisure, e.g. reading fiction.*	**ENTP** *Tend to need travel, adventure, unusual events.*
ENFJ *Tend to set up social events. Reading and the arts.*	**ENTJ** *Tend to organize groups, events that mix business and pleasure, competitive sports.*

showed it to friends). These perfect vacations are grouped by S–N and T–F rather than temperament, and illustrate well, if a little tongue in cheek, the ST desire for sensory experience, with variety for STPs and order for STJs, and so on. Negative reactions are valuable clues too.

THE TEMPERAMENTS

In theory, temperament should be more visible than the preferences. This is because Keirsey's theory focuses on what people do rather than on the hypothetical functions or preferences which are "unavoidably subjective, a matter of speculation and occasionally of

TABLE 10.3 (MBTI VACATIONS)

ISTJ *Gourmet's tour of France, savoring the delights of traditional vineyards (and grape crushing by foot), specialist fromageries and local cuisine.*

ISTP *Driving a modern, high-tech, all-amenities camper van around America's National Parks, with the freedom to experience the natural beauty in your own way.*

ESTP *White water rafting, bungee jumping and crocodile wrestling in OZ.*

ESTJ *Visiting Disneyland with the family, getting up at dawn to be the first in the queue, "doing" it all before it gets busy and then leaving to fit in another attraction before tea time.*

ISFJ *A well-earned week away with your true love in a Grade 2 listed building, sifting through the local antique shops.*

ISFP *Walking in Provence, experiencing the local culture, staying with local families, visiting markets and eating local cuisine.*

ESFP *Driving an old fashioned VW camper van to a rally with all the family, and having cook-outs with a large group of like-minded people.*

ESFJ *Italian cookery in Tuscany with practical lessons each morning, convivial lunches getting to know other course members and time to visit local sites and relax with new friends in the afternoons.*

(TABLE 10.3 *continued on next page*)

(TABLE 10.3 *continued from previous page*)

INFJ *The long-planned romantic week away in a rustic, rose-covered cottage in Dorset. Taking the Labrador for long walks with your significant other, and cosy evenings sipping wine in front of the log fire.*

INFP *Being alone with the elements to find yourself and meditate; exploring the coastline of NW Greenland at your own pace.*

ENFP *Staying in a large country house with a horde of friends, having extended discussions, playing games, and having many activities to choose from.*

ENFJ *Spiritual retreat on a Greek island, exploring new techniques of self-actualisation with a group of soul mates.*

INTJ *Visiting Boston to take a crash course in quantum mechanics at MIT.*

INTP *Visiting the Leonardo Museum in Vinci, staying in perfect, individual accommodation, perhaps in a room once occupied by a famous scientist.*

ENTP *Backpacking around the Middle East with the option of side trips to Turkey, Egypt and Milan, learning about the local cultures, creating stories to tell all your friends when you get home.*

ENTJ *Getting away from the pressures of work with a two-week intensive MBA course in a city where everything is happening.*

projection" (Keirsey 1998). However, observation, even though skilled and careful, is still subjective.

It is probably easier to observe someone's temperament accurately than it is their type, partly because of the greater emphasis on behavior but also because there are only four categories. The odds are better. However, there are still complicating factors. First, people are mixtures of the temperaments, with one predominating. Second, falsification of temperament seems possible, though perhaps less so than for type.

The behavioral clues for temperament follow from their characteristic motives. Thus:

- SPs, who primarily seek action and live in the present, tend to be calm in a crisis and to like taking risks and making and repairing things, to be energetic, casual, playful, and practical.

- SJs, who primarily seek order and closure, tend to be neat, traditional, and responsible, to be a source of stability, and to work before play. They like rules, clear objectives, and plans.

- NTs, who primarily seek competency, tend to create complex models of systems, to love debate for its own sake, and to focus on the future and on improving and redesigning everything, preferably at speed.

- NFs, who primarily seek identity or self-actualization, tend to empathize, and to seek harmony with other people and to be helpful and supportive to them, especially with time and ideas.

As I wrote the above, I think what a powerful and engaging set of ideas this is and how well they fit people I know, especially as a mixture, for example, Amarjit is 70 percent SJ, 20 percent NT, 8 percent NF, and 2 percent SP. But also, why has there been so little research to test them, both in general and as observational clues?

Please Understand Me II (Keirsey 1998) is packed with observations and speculations that, if true, are very valuable for observing temperament accurately. Some are also very specific. For example, SPs are said to:

- "Talk mostly of what is going on at the moment ... their everyday speech is typically filled with details and devoid of planning" (36).

- Have a pawing motion as their most common gesture.

- Use tools that get the job done with social approval a secondary consideration.

- Be "easily the most devil-may-care of all the types ... more subject to accidents" (47).

- Act on impulse more than to achieve security, autonomy, or authenticity.

SJs are said to:

- "Talk for the most part about the concrete particulars they observe in their material or social surroundings" (78).

- "Usually avoid showy hand gestures when they speak. But when they do get animated out come the hands: the index finger wags in warning.... and perhaps most familiar of all, SJs will bring one or both hands down in a chopping motion, to emphasize their statements or to cut off further discussion" (80).

- Be "creatures of habit, following faithfully the same routines in their daily lives" (92).

NTs are said to:

- "Talk little of what is observable, and much of what is imaginable. . . . ideas rather than objects" (165).

- "Try to avoid the irrelevant, the trivial, and the redundant. . . . reluctant to state the obvious. . . . unusually exacting about definitions" (165-66).

- "Prefer to appear unemotional when they communicate (and they can seem rather stiff)" (168).

- Use characteristic hand gestures that "express their need for precision and control. NTs make one or both hands into claws or talons, as if to seize the idea they are discussing. . . . use their fingers like a calculator, ticking off point after point. . . . and they will take small objects . . . to help map out their ideas. But perhaps the most telling gesture of all is the opposition of the thumb against the finger tips, as if the NT is bringing an idea or an argument to the finest possible point, and is savoring the precision" (168).

- Focus on "maximum results for minimum effort." "Efficiency is always the issue" (179).

- "Yearn for achievement" (188).

NFs are said to:

- "Talk little of what they observe" (120), tend to exaggerate and make intuitive leaps.

- "Extend their open hands to others, as if offering their counsel freely or accepting another's words as a gift. . . . or they will bring their hands together in various ways. . . . all as if trying to hold together two halves of a message" (122).

- Be unable not to "be personal" (137).

- Be "incurable romantics" (142).

The above are only a few examples of Keirsey's observations and ideas, and often he analyzes them further, eloquently and precisely. Barnum descriptions are sometimes a possibility, but in some of the most effective passages he contrasts the four temperaments, for example, "In their anticipation of things to come [SPs] are optimistic, expecting to get the breaks, [SJs] are pessimistic, expecting pitfalls, and [NFs] are credulous, expecting the best of people. [NTs] are strikingly different in their anticipations: they are skeptical, and thus expect all human endeavors, even their own, to be shot through with error" (180).

If the temperaments are "light years apart in their attitudes and actions" (Keirsey 1998, 18), and if the useful clues are as accessible as some of those listed above, then Keirsey's theory is a major contribution to personality research as well as to observing type more accurately. Keirsey is confident about his "convenient and remarkably accurate way of determining [their] temperament" (29), but is he right? He shows no interest in empirical evidence, but I think his ideas *demand* systematic, rigorous research to support, reject, or qualify them. The questions to investigate are obvious, for example, do most people use most of the gestures, or are some gestures indeed characteristic of each temperament? When are they used? Can they be distinguished readily by untrained observers? A key finding from the research on accuracy in person perception is that accurate judgments are based on several low validity cues and on patterns among them. This finding contradicts Keirsey's view, but his ideas have not been tested yet and could be a breakthrough.

A NOTE ON WHOLE TYPES

Some writers about type claim to observe "whole types" without going through stages. Nardi (1999), for example, uses the patterns and themes listed in Berens and Nardi (1999). An example of a pattern is "Discoverer Advocate," for ENFP "Discoverer" refers to how ENFPs tend to see themselves and Advocate to how others often see them (Berens and Nardi, 7). Several themes for each type are also listed such as, for ENFP, "Seek to have ideal relationships" and "Restless hunger for discovering their direction" (8). In contrast, of course, are ISTJs. Their pattern is called "Planner Inspector" and examples of their themes are "Getting work done first" and "Loyalty to their roles" (9).

This is an exciting possibility, which needs testing formally. If supported, it's a very significant contribution to understanding and describing the types and to the validity of the theory. However, it seems unlikely to be easy to train people to test it. Professions like osteopathy come to mind, in which for those who *can* develop it, a "feel" for diagnosing the nature of an injury is said to take two or three years.

CONCLUSIONS

We have good evidence for some clues for each preference but need a review of all the relevant evidence and studies of other possible clues.

There are many possible clues, so a further basis for choosing which ones to investigate is their importance in other respects—to increasing happiness or health or reducing conflict, for example. Money and leisure are two obvious possibilities. Keirsey's suggestions on clues for the temperaments seem to me very striking. If they're true, even to a fairly modest degree, they're a major breakthrough for personality theory and for applying MBTI theory.

Chapter 11

MBTI Practice and Research: Examples and Priorities for Research

*T*he many important *Myers Briggs Type Indicator® (MBTI®)* *applications include the broad areas of education, organ- izations, counseling, careers and multiculturalism (all reviewed in Hammer 1996 and Myers et al. 1998). More specific applications include love (Jones and Sherman 1997; Tieger and Barron-Tieger 2000), child rearing (Murphy 1992; Tieger and Barron-Tieger 1997), and time management (Fitzsimmons 1999). In this chapter I discuss three diverse applications of MBTI theory to illustrate further both its potential range and power and the need for evidence. The three areas of applications are ADHD, job performance, and sport. Finally, I suggest some priorities for MBTI research.*

ADHD

ADHD (attention deficit hyperactivity disorder) and ADD (attention deficit disorder) are vague and controversial labels (Alcock and Ryan 2000; Baldwin and Cooper 2000). At their most positive, the labels are attempts to diagnose an illness with a view to treating it and curing it, and at worst they are a socially accepted, convenient way of explaining and controlling difficult children, one which is highly profitable for drug companies. The behaviors or symptoms (if it is an illness) associated with ADHD include short attention span, inability to control impulses, crying and laughing a lot, and being easily bored, restless, and disruptive. Such behavior can, of course, put a great strain on relationships. Ritalin, the drug usually prescribed for ADHD, is a huge commercial success, and has been used for over 30 years. However, the evidence on its effectiveness and side effects seems to be mixed (Baldwin and Cooper 2000).

MBTI theory's relevance to ADHD is that it suggests the diagnosis is too easily made. It explains some, perhaps all, the behavior used to diagnose ADHD not as an illness but as characteristic of one of the temperaments, especially when a child is in an environment that clashes with that temperament. Sitting quietly most of the day doesn't suit everyone. Keirsey (1998) believes that a child who is bored by school in its usual form at this time in Western culture and wants excitement, action, and fun *now* (characteristics of the SP temperament in his theory) is a problem for many teachers, parents, guardians, and other children but a normal kind of personality. Moreover, the SP temperament is valued by society in adults, especially in certain careers.

Even if Keirsey's view is true for only some children diagnosed as having ADHD, it is critically important, for both ethical and practical reasons. Unfortunately, there are problems with testing it. The MBTI questionnaire is not appropriate for young children and the Murphy-Meisgeier Type Indicator for Children questionnaire has not yet been sufficiently validated for use with ADHD children. In any case, answering a questionnaire seems unlikely to hold the attention of young SPs, and studies using the Murphy Meisgeier have not given clear results (Alcock and Ryan 2000).

In a recent review, White (1999) found few studies of personality and ADHD. Children and adolescents (ages 7-21) with ADHD diagnoses seemed to be more likely than their peers to take risks. For example they are less likely to see severe consequences of risky behavior and report fewer attempts to prevent injury—consistent with Keirsey's views. There was also some support for a relationship between ADHD and the Big Five parallel of Perceiving, but like the risk-taking, this could at least partly be a reaction to the way they are expected to behave. Against Keirsey's view, there was also a suggestion from studies that children diagnosed as ADHD tend to be higher on the Big Five parallel of Intuition (White 1999).

A variety of treatments seem to be needed for ADHD symptoms in their extreme forms: "The complexity of the problem is such that it is unlikely that any single form of intervention will ever be appropriate for all cases of ADHD" (Baldwin and Cooper 2000, 602). Provost (1994) described working with several college students diagnosed when young as suffering from ADHD or ADD. She focused on helping them— they were ESTPs and ESFPs—develop their auxiliary T or F for greater balance and capacity for self-management. MBTI theory suggests some further specific practical advice, which seems worth testing, on how to treat children of SP temperament:

- exciting activities (and, less obviously, quiet, relaxing periods between)
- variety of activity (and not the same timetable each week)
- variety of group size (and some 1:1)
- feedback on performance and style as well as outcome
- movement
- more than one activity at a time
- family counseling
- skills training (e.g., of impulse control)

There are indications here too of a general problem for SPs in our current education system. As Myers et al. (1998) put it: "It would seem that the very things that are valued and used as criteria of educational success are quite opposite to the style and areas of competency of people with an SP temperament" (61). A related problem in the research on personality and job performance is discussed next.

JOB PERFORMANCE

MBTI theory predicts minor relationships between type and effectiveness at work, or job performance as it is usually referred to in the psychology literature. Such factors as type development, the amount of autonomy the particular job allows, interests, values, and the nature of the organization, in particular how formal its structure and rules are, will all play a part, and reduce the strength of straightforward correlations.

Empirically, the relationships found between personality and job performance have indeed been low. For example, the strongest correlation found by Barrick and Mount (1991) was about 0.2 with Conscientiousness, the Big Five characteristic corresponding to Judging. This relationship has been found for professionals, skilled/ semi-skilled workers, sales people, managers, and police officers. Salgado (1997) confirmed it and found an even lower relationship between

Extraversion and successful performance in jobs involving considerable interaction with others. In addition, Agreeableness—related to T–F—and Conscientiousness were also involved. Openness, related to S–N, was related, slightly, to training proficiency. From an MBTI perspective, the training proficiency relationship may be a function of training that is biased in favor of people with a preference for N and against those with a preference for S.

However, several general points are worth making about this area of research and application. First, correlations of 0.2 can be useful. Second, MBTI theory predicts how people work more than how well (in addition to such factors as choice of work). More subtly though, it also predicts which types will tend to be the *best* workers in particular occupations—a matter of talent plus motivation plus opportunity. Third, job performance has often been measured poorly, mainly by supervisors' ratings. On the other hand, it is difficult to devise good measures of job performance. Fourth, the relationships in this area are likely to be quite intricate ones (Mount and Barrick 1998; Judge et al. 1999), but they do exist. Fifth, some *components* of Conscientiousness may predict work performance or, rather, some aspects of work performance, better than others (Robertson et al. 2000). Robertson et al. argue for a more multifaceted view of both personality and work performance.

The Big Five interpretation of the "major finding" of a relationship between a preference for Judging (to use the MBTI term) and job performance is that "Individuals who are dependable, persistent, goal directed and organized tend to be higher performers on virtually any job; viewed negatively, those who are careless, irresponsible, low achievement striving and impulsive tend to be lower performers on virtually any job" (Mount and Barrick 1998, 851). For Mount and Barrick the practical implication is clear: "there are now two dispositional predictors in our field whose validity generalises: general mental ability and conscientiousness. Thus, no matter what job you are selecting for, if you want employees who will turn out to be good performers, you should hire those who work smarter and work harder" (856).

The MBTI interpretation of the relationship between Conscientiousness and effectiveness at work is in marked contrast. It finds that organizations following the advice based on Big Five research will miss the strengths of Ps, such as the trouble-shooting ability of SPs, their calmness and practical intelligence in a crisis. However, and fortunately, they may be saved to some extent by the imperfections of selection procedures and the versatility of applicants (Bayne 2004).

Recently there has been some movement in the psychology litera-. ture toward a more subtle and, from an MBTI perspective, a more accurate and balanced view, for example that rebelliousness and flexibility can be useful characteristics in some work situations, and that "some of the characteristics associated with high conscientiousness [preference for Judging] may also serve to undermine certain aspects of managerial performance" (Robertson et al. 2000, 173)—quite close to MBTI theory. However, this more positive conception of low Conscientiousness, as well as a slightly more critical view of high Conscientiousness, is not apparent in Judge et al.'s (1999) major study, or in the literature on job performance generally. A very similar bias from an MBTI point of view, in counseling, is that people low on Conscientiousness make poor clients (Miller 1991; Muten 1991; Bayne 2004).

SPORT

Niednagel (1997) suggests, with confidence, that each of the types is most likely to excel at different sports, or different positions in a particular sport, and that, conversely, "it tends to be wasteful and discouraging to persist with the wrong sport or position for your type." He sees the four SF types as "gross motor skilled," STs as "fine motor skilled," NFs as "language skilled," and NTs as "logical abstraction skilled" (46–47). Gross motor skills use arms, legs, and torsos. Fine motor skills refer especially to eye-hand coordination. His view here is that STJs specialize in *dexterity* (using eyes and hands to manipulate objects skillfully), while STPs are potentially best at *positioning* (putting the hand in the right place at the right moment).

Niednagel is appropriately careful about his view of the relationship between potential and actual, and the role of upbringing and present environment. For example: "an NF athlete who practices a lot more than the ST can develop a greater skill in fine motor movements. However, the ST athlete who practices as much as the non-ST will develop the greatest fine motor proficiency of all the types. STs have the greatest potential for excellence with hand-eye coordination and other fine motor skills" (77). This echoes Myers's general view of gifts and who will develop them most (Myers with Myers 1980).

Niednagel's rationale for links between sporting prowess and language skills (NF) and logical abstraction skills (NT) are not clear to me. However, I found many interesting hypotheses:

1) NFs are the group whose performance is most likely to be affected by mood (78).

2) "Most athletes, if they knew the brain's functioning, and then could choose a Brain Type, would choose ISTP" (281).

3) "ESTJs need to consciously relax their arms, wrists and hands in pressured competition. Otherwise, their superior fine motor skills will work counterproductively" (307).

Niednagel's views are based so far on anecdotes and testimonials. Brain-mapping techniques (Barnes, 1998), which Niednagel refers to, may give us a better idea of how valid they are and be relevant to testing aspects of type dynamics and type development. Some of Niednagel's ideas on coaching are more firmly based in type theory and current research but still need to be formally tested, for example, his view that each type responds best to different styles of coaching. Thus, "SFs learn best from practical and simple teaching, emphasizing how the body movements are performed" (76), but whereas SFJs need a step-by-step approach, SFPs need and take to a holistic one. Therefore, SFPs, and Ps generally, he argues, tend to be more rhythmic and flowing.

CONCLUDING REMARKS

The issues for MBTI theory and practice that I've discussed in this book are a small proportion of those which could be investigated, and even so would take many research-years. This has two implications. First, when applying type, we have for the most part to rely on beliefs and expert judgment until other levels of evidence are better (Bayne 2004). Second, individual researchers, and to some extent journal editors and reviewers, can *influence,* but definitely not prescribe, the topics which are investigated, as can publications, including, I hope, this one.

My view of priorities for MBTI research—of the *most* interesting, useful, and valuable issues to study from those already highly selected for review in this book—is below. However, I also like the idea that researchers should do "silly" studies from time to time and Skinner's first principle of research: "if you find something interesting, drop everything else."

Priorities for research

1) Type dynamics, preferably as straightforwardly and directly as possible. I hope its neglect isn't significant. Why haven't the easiest ways to test it been pursued? Can we find evidence that is clear, relatively tangible, and engaging? Biology (behavioral genetics and neuropsychology) may be very relevant here but won't replace psychology.

2) Temperament, because it seems both relatively simple and very powerful in predicting behavior: an extraordinary combination given the history of personality research.

3) Type development, particularly a valid measure.

4) Underlying considerations for applying MBTI theory, in particular:

   a) the best cues or clues for observing type accurately. These are very relevant to refining and teaching the theory too.

   b) the most effective approaches to verifying type, and therefore evaluation of success and of frameworks and specific exercises, because this is the area in which MBTI theory has the most general impact.

5) Some specific applications, either because of their potential for redressing grave social injustices, as in misdiagnosing SPs as having ADHD and selecting Js for jobs in which Ps would tend to work more effectively, or because of their impact on the greatest number of people.

REFERENCES

Abella, K. and S. Dutton. 1995. Using diversity to teach diversity. 23½ different ways to introduce the MBTI preferences. *Proceedings of APT XI* 83-84 Kansas City MO: Association for Psychological Type.

Alcock, M.W. and P. M. Ryan. 2000. ADD, type, teaching and learning. *Journal of Psychological Type* 52: 5-10.

Allen, J. and S. A. Brock. 2000. *Health Care Communication and Personality Type.* London: Routledge.

Ambady, N. and R. Rosenthal. 1993. Half a minute: Teacher evaluations from thin slices of nonverbal behavior and physical attractiveness. *Journal of Personality* and Social *Psychology* 64: 431-41.

Argyle, M. 1996. *The Social Psychology of Leisure* London: Penguin.

Aron, E. N. 1999. High sensitivity as one source of fearfulness and shyness. In L. A. Schmidt and J. Schulkin, eds., *Extreme Fear, Shyness, and Social Phobia: Origins, Biological Mechanisms and Clinical Outcomes.* Oxford: Oxford University Press.

Aron, E. N. and A. Aron. 1997. Sensory-processing sensitivity and its relation to introversion and emotionality. *Journal of Personality and Social Psychology* 73: 345-68.

Ashton, M. C., K. Lee, and S. V. Paunonen. 2002. What is the central feature of Extraversion? Social attention versus reward sensitivity. *Journal of Personality and Social Psychology* 83: 245-52.

Aspendorpf, J. B., and S. Wilpers. 1998. Personality effects on social relationships. *Journal of Personality and Social Psychology* 74: 1531-44.

Baldwin, S. and P. Cooper. 2000. How should ADHD be treated? *The Psychologist* 13: 598-602.

Barbuto, J. E., and B. A. Plummer. 2000. Mental boundaries and Jung's psychological types: A Profile Analysis. *Journal of Psychological Type* 54: 17-21.

Barnes, C. B. 1998. The modular brain and psychological type. *Bulletin of Psychological Type* 21: 4-5.

Barnes, C. B. 2001. Genetics and psychological type. *Bulletin of Psychological Type* 24: 32-33.

Barrick, M. R. and M. K. Mount. 1991. The big five personality dimensions and job performance: A meta-analysis. *Personnel Psychology* 44: 1-26.

Bathurst, J. 2000. The relationship between reported type and best-fit type: Evidence for administrator bias? *Journal of Psychological Type* 54: 5-11.

Bayne, R. 1988. Accuracy in judging the four attitudes. *Journal of Psychological Type* 16: 61-66.

Bayne, R. 1995. *The Myers-Briggs Indicator: A Critical Review and Practical Guide*. Cheltenham: Nelson Thornes.

Bayne, R. 2004. *Psychological Types at Work: An MBTI Perspective*. London: Thomson.

Bayne, R. and F. O'Neill. 1988. Handwriting and personality: An empirical test of expert graphologists' judgments. *Guidance and Assessment Review* 4: 1-3.

Bayne, R. and R. Kwiatkowski. 1998. Type and time orientation: A partial replication and critique of Harrison and Lawrence. *Journal of Psychological Type* 47: 28-34.

Bem, D. J. 1983. Constructing a theory of the triple typology: Some (second) thoughts on nomothetic and idiographic approaches to personality. *Journal of Personality* 51: 566-77.

Berens, L. V. 1999. *Dynamics of Personality Type: Understanding and applying Jung's cognitive processes*. Huntingdon Beach CA: Telos Publications.

Berens, L. V. 2000. *Understanding Yourself and Others: An introduction to temperament*. Huntingdon Beach CA: Telos Publications.

Berens, L. V. 2001. *Understanding Yourself and Others: An introduction to interaction styles*. Huntingdon Beach CA: Telos Publications.

Berens, L. V. and D. Nardi. 1999. *The Sixteen Personality Types, Descriptions for Self-Discovery*. Huntingdon Beach CA: Telos Publications.

Binning, J. F., J. M. LeBreton, and A. J. Adorno. 1999. Assessing personality. In R. W. Eder and M. M. Harris, eds., *The Employment Interview Handbook*. 2nd ed. London: Sage.

Block, J. 1995. A contrarian view of the Five-Factor approach to personality description. *Psychological Review* 117: 187-215.

Boice, R. 1994. *How Writers Journey to Comfort and Fluency: A Psychological Adventure*. London: Prager.

Bond, T. 2000. *Standards and Ethics for Counselling in Action*. 2nd ed. London: Sage.

Bouchard, T. J. and Y-M. Hur. 1998. Genetic and environmental influences on the continuous scales of the Myers-Briggs Type Indicator: An analysis based on twins reared apart. *Journal of Personality* 66: 135-49.

Brenstein, E. 1996. Diversity in work styles. In F.T.L. Leong and J. T. Austin, eds., *The Psychology Research Handbook*. London: Sage.

Brock, S. A. 1994. *Using Type in Selling*. Palo Alto CA: CPP.

Brock, S. A. and J. Allen. 2000. Working with type in health care: Same words, different meanings? *Journal of Psychological Type* 53: 4-10.

Broer, E. and N. G. McCarley. 1999. Using and validating the Myers-Briggs Type Indicator in China. *Journal of Psychological Type* 51: 5-12.

Brownsword, A. 1987. *It Takes All Types!* Fairfax CA: Baytree Publication Co.

Carr, S. 1997. *Type Clarification: Finding the Fit.* Oxford: OPP.

Cauvin, P. and G. Cailloux. 1999. An S/N exercise. *Bulletin of Psychological Type* 22: 30-32.

Cheek, J. M. and A. H. Buss. 1981. Shyness and sociability. *Journal of Personality and Social Psychology* 41: 330-99.

Churchill, S. and R. Bayne. 1998. Psychological type and different conceptions of empathy in experienced counsellors. *Counselling Psychology Quarterly* 11: 379-90.

Churchill, S. and R. Bayne. 2001. Psychological type and conceptions of empathy in experienced counsellors: Qualitative results. *Counselling Psychology Quarterly* 14: 203-17.

Clifford, B. R. 2003. Research: The ubiquitous handmaiden of professionalism. In R. Bayne and I. Horton, eds., *Applied Psychology. Current Issues and New Directions.* London: Sage.

Cohen, J. 1988. *Statistical Power Analysis for the Behavioural Sciences.* 2nd ed. Hillsdale NF: Erlbaum.

Cohen, J. 1990. Things I have learned so far. *American Psychologist* 45: 1304-12.

Cohen, J. 1994. The earth is round. *American Psychologist* 49: 997-1003.

Costa, P. T. and R. R. McCrae. 1992a. Four ways five factors are basic. *Personality and Individual Differences* 13: 653-65.

Costa, P. T. and R. R. McCrae. 1992b. The NEO PI-R *Professional Manual.* Odessa FL: Psychological Assessment Resources.

Costa, P. T. and R. R. McCrae. 1998. Six approaches to the explication of facet-level traits: Examples from Conscientiousness. *European Journal of Personality* 12: 117-34.

Crozier, W. R. 2002. Shyness. *The Psychologist* 15: 460-63.

Dahlstrom, W. G. 1995. Pigeons, people and pigeon-holes. *Journal of Personality Assessment* 64: 2-20.

Deary, I. J., H. Ramsay, J. A. Wilson, and M. Raid. 1988. Stimulated salivation: Correlations with personality and time of day effects. *Personality and Individual Differences* 9: 903-9.

Delunas, E. 1992. *Survival Games Personalities Play.* Carmel CA: Sunflower Ink.

DePaulo, B. M. 1993. The ability to judge others from their expressive behaviours. In K. H. Craik, R. Hogan, and R. N. Wolfe, eds., *Fifty Years of Personality Psychology.* London: Plenum.

Diamantopoulos, A. and B. B. Schlegelmilch. 1997. *Taking the Fear out of Data Analysis. A step-by-step approach.* London: Dryden Press.

DiTiberio, J. K. and A. L. Hammer. 1993. *Introduction to Type in College.* Palo Alto CA: CPP.

DiTiberio, J. K. and G. H. Jensen. 1995. *Writing and Personality.* Palo Alto CA: Davies-Black.

Duan, C. and C. E. Hill. 1996. The current state of empathy research. *Journal of Counselling Psychology* 11: 379-90.

Dunning, D. 2003. *Introduction to Type and Communication.* Palo Alto CA: CPP.

Ennis, R. H. 1987. A taxonomy of critical thinking dispositions and abilities. In J. B. Baron and R. J. Sternberg, eds., *Teaching Thinking Skills: Theory and Practice.* New York: Freeman.

Epstein, S. 1997. This I have learned from over 40 years of personality research. *Journal of Personality* 65: 3-32.

Eysenck, H. J. 1973. *Eysenck on Extraversion.* New York: Wiley.

Eysenck, H. J. 1992. Four ways five factors are not basic. *Personality and Individual Differences* 13: 667-73.

Fields, M. U. and J. B. Reid. 1999. *Shape Up Your Program! Tips, Teasers and Thoughts for Type Trainers.* Gainesville FL: CAPT.

Fitzsimmons, S. 1999. *Type and time management.* Edmonton: Psychometrics Canada Ltd.

Fletcher, C. 1981. Candidates' beliefs and self-presentation strategies in selection interviews. *Personnel Review* 10: 14-17.

Forer, B. R. 1949. The fallacy of personal validation: A classroom demonstration. *Journal of Abnormal and Social Psychology* 44: 118-23.

Friedman, H. S., J. S. Tucker, C. Tomlinson-Keasey, et al. 1993. Does childhood personality predict longevity? *Journal of Personality and Social Psychology* 65: 176-185.

Frisbie, G. R. 1988. Cognitive styles: An alternative to Keirsey's temperaments. *Journal of Psychological Type* 16: 13-21.

Funder, D. C. 1995. On the accuracy of personality judgment: A realistic approach. *Psychological Review* 102: 652-70.

Funder, D. C. 1997. *The Personality Puzzle.* London: W.W. Norton.

Funder, D. C. 1999. *Personality Judgment. A Realistic Approach to Person Perception.* London: Academic Press.

Funder, D. C. 2001. Personality. *Annual Review of Psychology* 52: 197-221.

Funder, D. C. and C. D. Sneed. 1993. Behavioral manifestations of personality: An ecological approach to judgemental accuracy. *Journal of Personality and Social Psychology* 64: 479-90.

Furnham, A. 1996. The big five versus the big four: The relationship between the Myers-Briggs Type Indicator (MBTI) and NEO-PI five factor model of personality. *Personality and Individual Differences* 21: 303-7.

Furnham, A. and P. Heaven. 1999. *Personality and Social behavior.* London: Arnold.

Furnham, A. and S. Schofield. 1987. Accepting personality test feedback: A review of the Barnum effect. *Current Psychology Research and Reviews* 6: 162-78.

Garden, A. M. 1991. Unresolved issues with the Myers-Briggs Type Indicator. *Journal of Psychological Type* 22: 3-14.

Goldberg, L. R. 1992. The development of markers for the big-five factor structure. *Psychological Assessment* 4: 26-42.

Goldberg, L. R. 1993. The structure of phenotypic personality traits. *American Psychologist* 48: 26-34.

Govier, E. 1998. Brainsex and occupation. In J. K. Radford, ed., *Gender and Choice in Education and Occupation.* London: Routledge.

Graziano, W. G. and N. Eisenberg. 1997. Agreeableness: A dimension of personality. In R. Hogan, J. A. Johnson, and S. Briggs, eds., *Handbook of Personality Psychology.* San Diego CA: Academic Press.

Haase, R. F., D. M. Waechter, and G. S. Solomon. 1982. How significant is a significant difference? Average effect size of research in counselling psychology. *Journal of Counselling Psychology* 29: 58-65.

Hallows, L. 1999. Correlation of psychological preferences using hand analysis and MBTI results. *APT XIII International Conference Proceedings* 279-88. Kansas City MO: Association for Psychological Type.

Hammer, A. L. ed. 1996. *MBTI Application: A Decade of Research on the Myers-Briggs Type Indicator.* Palo Alto CA: CPP.

Harker, J. B., J. H. Reyneirse, and L. Komisin. 1998. Independent observer ratings and the correlates of MBTI preferences with their behavioral descriptors. *Journal of Psychological Type* 45: 5-20.

Harper, D., M. R. Mulvey, and M. Robinson. 2003. Beyond evidence-based practice: Rethinking the relationship between research, theory and practice. In R. Bayne and I. Horton, eds., *Applied Psychology. Current Trends and New Directions.* London: Sage.

Harrison, D. and G. Lawrence. 1985. Psychological type and time orientation: Do middle school students differ in projecting their personal futures? *Journal of Psychological Type* 9: 10-15.

Harrison, T. D. 1998. Quick and clean: Using easel activities to introduce type in a limited time frame. *Journal of Psychological Type* 45: 39-44.

Harvey, R. J. 1996. Reliability and validity. In A. L. Hammer, ed., *MBTI Applications: A Decade of Research on the Myers-Briggs Type Indicator.* Palo Alto CA: CPP.

Hayman, C. H. and M. Allen. 1997. How to introduce type to high school students: Methods that work and what we've learned. *Proceedings of APT XI* 61-64. Kansas City MO: Association for Psychological Type.

Hedges, L. V. 1987. How hard is hard science, how soft is soft science: The empirical cumulativeness of research. *American Psychologist* 42: 443-45.

Heinrich, K. T. and C. A. Pfeiffer. 1989. Using the MBTI to personalize the teaching of interviewing skills. *Proceedings of the Eighth Biennial International Conference of the Association for Psychological Type*, 77-81. Kansas City MO: Association for Psychological Type.

Hicks, L. E. 1984. Conceptual and empirical analysis of some assumptions of an explicitly typological theory. *Journal of Personality and Social Psychology* 46: 1118-31.

Hinnen, D. A. 1994. Gifts preferring: Type bias in *Gifts Differing. Journal of Psychological Type* 29: 3-5.

Hinrichs, J. R. 1976. Personnel training. In M. D. Dunnette, ed. *Handbook of Industrial and Organisational Psychology.* Chicago: Rand McNally.

Hirsh, S. K. 1992. *Using the Myers-Briggs Type Indicator in Organizations.* 2nd ed. Palo Alto CA: Consulting Psychologists Press.

Hirsh, S. K. and J. M. Kummerow. 1989. *Life Types.* New York: Warner Books.

Jeffries, B. 1991. *True to Type.* Norfolk VA: Hampton Roads.

Jensen, G. H. and J. K. DiTiberio. 1989. *Personality and the Teaching of Composition.* Norwood NJ: Ablex Publishing Corporation.

John, O. P. and R. W. Robins. 1994. Traits and types, dynamics and development: No doors should be closed in the study of personality. *Psychological Inquiry* 5: 137-42.

Johnson, J. R. 2002. Research and the MBTI. *Bulletin of Psychological Type* 25: 28-29.

Jones, J. K. and R. G. Sherman. 1997. *Intimacy and Type.* Gainesville FL: CAPT.

Joseph, J. 2003. The Gene Illusion: *Genetic Research in Psychology and Psychiatry under the Microscope.* Ross-on-Wye: PCCS Books.

Judge, T. A., C. A. Higgins, C. J. Thoresen, and M. A. Barrick. 1999. The Big Five personality traits, general mental ability, and career success across the life span. *Personnel Psychology* 52: 621-52.

Jung, C. G. 1923. *Psychological Types.* London: Routledge.

Keefer, K. H. 1995. Using guided imagery for type development II: A case study. *Journal of Psychological Type* 33: 11-18.

Keefer, K. H. and W. W. Yabroff. 1995. Using guided imagery for type development I: The Yabroff method. *Journal of Psychological Type* 33: 3-10.

Keirsey, D. 1998. *Please Understand Me II.* Del Mar CA: Prometheus Nemesis.

Keirsey, D. and M. Bates. 1978. *Please Understand Me.* 3rd ed. Del Mar, CA: Prometheus Nemesis.

Kenrick, D. and D. C. Funder. 1988. Profiting from controversy: Lessons from the person-situation debate. *American Psychologist* 43: 23-34.

Kihlstrom, J. F. 1999. The psychological unconscious. In L. A. Pervin and O. P. John, eds. *Handbook of Personality: Theory and Research.* London: Guilford Press.

Kise, J. A. G. and B. Russell. 2001. Introducing type in middle schools. *APT XIV Conference Proceedings*. Kansas City. MO: Association for Psychological Type.

Kroeger, O. and J. M. Thuesen. 1988. *Type Talk*. New York: Delacorte Press.

Kroeger, O. with J. M. Thuesen. 1992. *Type Talk at Work*. New York: Delacorte Press.

Kroeger, O. and J. M. Thuesen. 1994. *16 Ways to Love Your Lover*. New York: Delacorte Press.

Kummerow, J. M. 2001. Examining type bias and inclusivity: Lessons from ethnic identity viewpoints. *Journal of Psychological Type* 56: 6-9.

Kummerow, J. M. and N. L. Quenk. 1992. *Interpretive Guide for the MBTI Extended Analysis Report*. Palo Alto CA: Consulting Psychologists Press.

Kummerow, J. M. and N. L. Quenk. 2003. *Understanding Your MBTI Step II Results*. Palo Alto CA: Consulting Psychologists Press.

Lawrence, G. D. 1993. *People Types and Tiger Stripes*. 3rd ed. Gainesville FL: CAPT.

Lawrence, G. D. 1997. *Looking at Type and Learning Styles*. Gainesville FL: CAPT.

Lawrence, G. D. 1998. *Descriptions of the Sixteen Types*. Gainesville FL: CAPT.

Lawrence, G. D. and C. R. Martin. 2001. *Building People, Building Programs*. Gainesville FL: CAPT.

Leong, F. T. L. and J. T. Austin, eds. 1996. *The Psychology Research Handbook*. London: Sage.

Ley, P. 1988. *Communicating with Patients*. London: Croom Helm.

Lieberman, M. D. and R. Rosenthal. 2001. Why introverts can't always tell who likes them: Multi-tasking and nonverbal decoding. *Journal of Personality and Social Psychology* 80: 294-310.

Linder, R. 2000a. Which way to the good life? *Bulletin of Psychological Type* 23: 4-6.

Linder, R. 2000b. *What Will I Do With My Money? How Your Personality Affects Your Financial Behavior*. Chicago, IL: Northfield.

Lively, P. 1998. *Spiderweb*. London: Penguin.

Loehlin, J. C., R. R. McCrae, P. T. Costa, and O. P. John. 1998. Heritabilities of common and measure-specific components of the Big Five personality factors. *Journal of Research in Personality* 32: 431-453

Loomis, A. B. 1999. *Write From the Start*. Gainesville FL: CAPT.

Lucas, R. E., E. Diener, A. Grob, E. M. Suh, and L. Shao. 2000. Cross-cultural evidence for the fundamental features of extraversion. *Journal of Personality and Social Psychology* 79: 452-68.

Luzader, M. 2001. Applying type to communication. *Journal of Psychological Type* 56: 37-39.

Lykken, D. T., M. McGue, A. Tellegen, and T. J. Bouchard Jr. 1992. Emergenesis: Genetic traits that may not run in families. *American Psychologist* 47: 1565-77.

Marlowe, J. 1998. Presenting type dynamically. *Journal of Psychological Type* 47: 35-41.

Martin, C. R. 1997. *Looking at Type: The Fundamentals.* Gainesville FL: CAPT.

Matthews, G. and G. Deary. 1998. *Personality Traits.* Cambridge: Cambridge University Press.

McAdams, D. P. 1992. The five-factor model in personality: A critical appraisal. *Journal of Personality* 60: 329-61.

McAdams, D. P. 1995. What do we know when we know a person? *Journal of Personality* 63: 365-96.

McAdams, D. P. 1998. Trick or treat: Clarifying concepts and accounting for human individuality. *Psychological Inquiry* 9: 54-157.

McAdams, D. P. 2001. *The Person: An Integrated Introduction to Personality Psychology.* London: Harcourt.

McCarley, N. G. and T. G. Carskadon. 1986. The perceived accuracy of elements of the 16 type descriptions of Myers and Keirsey among men and women: Which elements are most accurate, should the type descriptions be different for men and women, and do the type descriptions stereotype Sensing types? *Journal of Psychological Type* 11: 2-29.

McCarley, N. G. and T. G. Carskadon. 1987. Findings and strategies leading to empirically based type descriptions. *Journal of Psychological Type* 13: 9-14.

McCaulley, M. 1996. Traversing the SN chasm. *Bulletin of Psychological Type* 19: 22-24.

McCrae, R. 1994a. New goals for trait psychology. *Psychological Inquiry* 5: 148-53.

McCrae, R. 1994b. Openness to experience: expanding the boundaries of Factor V. *European Journal of Personality* 8: 251-72.

McCrae, R. 1996. Integrating the levels of personality. *Psychological Inquiry* 7: 353-56.

McCrae, R. R. and P. R. Costa Jr. 1983. Social desirability scales: More substance than style. *Journal of Consulting and Clinical Psychology* 51: 882-88.

McCrae, R. R. and P. T. Costa. 1989. Re-interpreting the Myers-Briggs Type Indicator from the perspective of the five factor model of personality. *Journal of Personality* 57: 17-37.

McLeod, J. 1999. *Practitioner Research in Counselling.* London: Sage.

McLeod, J. 2001. *Qualitative Research in Counselling and Psychotherapy.* London: Sage.

Mendelsohn, G. A., D. S. Weiss, and N. R. Feimer. 1982. Conceptual and empirical analysis of the typological implications of patterns of socialization and femininity. *Journal of Personality and Social Psychology* 42: 1157-70.

Merrill, M. D. 1983. Component display theory. In C. M. Reigeluth, ed., *Instructional Design Theories and Models: An Overview of Their Current Status.* Hillsdale NJ: Lawrence Erlbaum.

Miller, E. M. 1997. Could nonshared environmental variance have evolved to assure diversification through randomness? *Evolution and Human Behavior* 18: 195-221.

Miller, T. R. 1991. The psychotherapeutic utility of the five-factor model of personality: A clinician's experience. *Journal of Personality Assessment* 57: 415-33.

Mitchell, W. D. 1991. A test of type theory using the TDI. *Journal of Psychological Type* 22: 15-26.

Mitchell, W. D. with N. L. Quenk and J. M. Kummerow. 1997. *MBTI Step II: A Description of the Subscales.* Palo Alto CA: Consulting Psychologists Press.

Mitroff, I. and R. Kilmann. 1978. *Methodological Approaches to Social Science: Integrating divergent concepts and theories.* San Francisco: Jossey-Bass.

Mount, M. K. and M. R. Barrick. 1998. Five reasons why the "Big Five" article has been frequently cited. *Personnel Psychology* 51: 849-857.

Murphy, E. 1992. *The Developing Child: Using Jungian Type to Understand Children.* Palo Alto CA: Consulting Psychologists Press.

Murray, W. D. G. 1995. *Give Yourself the Unfair Advantage.* Gladwyne PA: Type and Temperament.

Muten, E. 1991. Self-reports, spouse ratings, and psychophysiological assessment in a behavioural medicine program: An application of the five-factor model *Journal of Personality Assessment* 57: 449-69.

Myers, I. B. 1976. *Introduction to Type.* 2nd ed. Palo Alto CA: Consulting Psychologists Press.

Myers, I. B. 1998. *Introduction to Type.* 6th ed. Palo Alto CA: CPP.

Myers, I. B. with P. B. Myers 1980. *Gifts Differing.* Palo Alto CA: Consulting Psychologists Press.

Myers, I. B., M. H. McCaulley, N. L. Quenk, and A. L. Hammer. 1998. *MBTI Manual: A Guide to the Development and Use of the Myers-Briggs Type Indicator.* 3rd ed. Palo Alto CA: Consulting Psychologists Press.

Myers, K. D. 1993. Isabel Briggs Myers and type development. *Bulletin of Psychological Type* 16: 6-8.

Myers, K. D. and L. K. Kirby. 1994. *Introduction to Type Dynamics and Type Development.* Palo Alto CA: Consulting Psychologists Press.

Myers, K. D., N. L. Quenk, and L. K. Kirby. 1995. The MBTI comfort-discomfort dimension is not a measure of NEO-PI neuroticism: A position paper. *Journal of Psychological Type* 35: 3-9.

Myers, S. 1995. *Influencing People Using Myers-Briggs*. Wirral, West Kirby: Team Technology.

Myers, S. 1997. Illuminating type dynamics. *Bulletin of Psychological Type* 20: 38-40.

Myers, S. 2001. Using the MTR-I alongside the MBTI. *Proceedings of APT XIV International Conference,* 169-182. Kansas City MO: Association for Psychological Type. Available on-line at www.mtr-i.com.

Nardi, D. 1999. *Character and Personality Type: Discovering Your Uniqueness for Career and Relationship Success.* Huntingdon Beach CA: Telos Publications.

Niednagel, J. P. 1997. *Your Key to Sports Success.* Laguna Niguel CA: Laguna Press.

Patrick, J. 1992. *Training: Research and Practice.* London: Academic Press.

Patrick, J. 2000. Training. In N. Chmiel, ed. *Introduction to Work and Organizational Psychology: A European Perspective.* Oxford: Blackwell.

Paunonen, S. V. and M. C. Ashton. 2001. Big Five factors and facets and the prediction of behavior. *Journal of Personality and Social Psychology* 81: 524-39.

Pearman, R. R. and S. C. Albritton. 1997. *I'm Not Crazy: I'm Just Not You.* Palo Alto CA: Davies-Black.

Pearman, R. R. and J. Fleenor. 1996. Differences in observed and self-reported qualities of psychological types. *Journal of Psychological Type* 39: 3-17.

Pennebaker, J. W. and L. A. King. 1999. Linguistic styles: Language use as an individual difference. *Journal of Personality and Social Psychology* 77: 1296-1312.

Pennebaker, J. W. and T. C. Lay. 2002. Language and personality during crisis: Analyses of Mayor Rudolph Giuliani's press conferences. *Journal of Research in Personality* 36: 271-82.

Plomin, R. 2001. Genetics and behavior. *The Psychologist* 14: 134-39.

Pratt, C. D. and P. Gray. 1999. Bridging the SN Chasm. *APT XIII Conference Proceedings,* 227-28. Scottsdale AZ: Association for Psychological Type.

Pratt, C. D. and P. Gray. 2001. Blending logic and values in the workplace. *APT XIV Conference Proceeding,* 95-97. Minneapolis MN: Association for Psychological Type.

Provost, J. 1994. ADHD, ADD, and psychological type. *Bulletin of Psychological Type* 17: 8-10.

Provost, J. A. 1990. *Work, Play and Type.* Palo Alto CA: Consulting Psychologists Press.

Provost, J. A. 1993. *Applications of the Myers-Briggs Type Indicator in Counseling: A Casebook.* 2nd ed. Gainesville FL: CAPT.

Quenk, N. L. 1993. *Beside Ourselves: Our Hidden Personality in Everyday Life.* Palo Alto CA: Consulting Psychologists Press.

Quenk, N. L. 1996. *In the Grip: Our Hidden Personality.* Palo Alto CA: Consulting Psychologists Press.

Quenk, N. L. 2000. *Essentials of Myers-Briggs Type Indicator Assessment.* Chichester: Wiley.

Quenk, N. L. 2002. *Was That Really Me?* Palo Alto CA: Davies-Black.

Quenk, N. L. and W. D. Mitchell. 1997. Is everyone a type? *APT XII International Conference Proceedings,* 135–38. Boston MA: Association for Psychological Type.

Quenk, N. L., A. L. Hammer, and M. Majors. 2001. *MBTI Step II Manual.* Palo Alto CA: Consulting Psychologists Press.

Rakos, R. F. 1991. *Assertive behavior: Theory, Research and Training.* London: Routledge.

Reynierse, J. H. 2000. The combination of preferences and the formation of MBTI types. *Journal of Psychological Type* 52: 18–31.

Reynierse, J. H. and J. B. Harker. 2000. Waiting for Godot, the search for the Holy Grail, and the futility of obtaining meaningful whole-type effects. *Journal of Psychological Type* 53: 11–18.

Reynierse, J. H. and J. B. Harker. 2001a. The interactive and addictive nature of psychological type. *Journal of Psychological Type* 58: 6–32.

Reynierse, J. H. and J. B. Harker. 2001b. Social acceptability of natural language descriptors associated with the MBTI preferences. *Journal of Psychological Type* 59: 29–35.

Robertson, I. J., H. Baron, P. Gibbons, R. MacIver and G. Nyfield. 2000. Conscientiousness and managerial performance. *Journal of Occupational and Organizational Psychology* 73: 171–80.

Robinson, D. C. 2001. Learning styles in the 21st century for a global community. In *APT XIV Conference Proceedings,* 195–212. Kansas City MO: Association for Psychological Type.

Robson, C. 2002. *Real World Research.* 2nd ed. Oxford: Blackwell.

Ruhl, D. L. and R. F. Rodgers. 1992. The perceived accuracy of the 16 type descriptions of Myers and Keirsey: A replication of McCarley and Carskadon. *Journal of Psychological Type* 23: 22–26.

Rutledge, D. H. 1999. Typewatching: What to look for and who cares. *Proceedings of APT XIII,* 191–200. Kansas City MO: Association for Psychological Type.

Rutter, M. and R. Plomin. 1997. Opportunities for psychiatry from genetic findings. *British Journal of Psychiatry* 171: 209–219.

Ryan, P. 2001. The power of type in the search for identity. *Bulletin of Psychological Type* 24: 16–19.

Rytting, M., R. Ware, and R. A. Prince. 1994. Bimodal distributions in a sample of CEOs: Validating evidence for the MBTI. *Journal of Psychological Type* 31: 16–23.

Salas, E. and J. A. Cannon-Bowers. 2001. The science of training: A decade of progress. *Annual Review of Psychology* 52: 471-99.

Salgado, J. F. 1997. The five factor model of personality and job performance in the European community. *Journal of Applied Psychology* 82: 30-43.

Scherer, K. R. 1979. Nonlinguistic indicators of emotion and psychopathology. In C. E. Izard, ed., *Emotions in Personality and Psychopathology*. New York: Plenum.

Seegmiller, R. A. and D. L. Epperson. 1987. Distinguishing thinking-feeling preferences through the content analysis of natural language. *Journal of Personality Assessment* 51: 42-52.

Sheldon, K. M., A. J. Elliot, K. Youngmee, and T. Kasser. 2001. What is satisfying about satisfying events? Testing 10 candidate psychological needs. *Journal of Personality and Social Psychology* 80: 325-39.

Shields, C. 1976. *Small Ceremonies*. London: Fourth Estate.

Shields, C. 1977. *The Box Garden*. London: Fourth Estate.

Smith, J. B. 1993. Teachers' grading styles: the languages of Thinking and Feeling. *Journal of Psychological Type* 26: 37-41.

Spinelli, E. 2001. *The Mirror and the Hammer: Challenges to therapeutic orthodoxy*. London: Continuum.

Spoto, A. 1995. *Jung's Typology in Perspective*. 2nd ed. Wilmette IL: Chiron Publications.

Tavris, C., and C. Wade. 1993. *Psychology*. 3rd ed. London: HarperCollins.

Thayer, R. E. 1996. *The Origin of Everyday Moods. Managing energy, tension and stress*. Oxford: Oxford University Press.

Thompson, H. L. 1996a. *Jung's Function–Attitudes Explained*. Watkinsville GA: Wormhole Publications.

Thompson, H. L. 1996b. "Natural" reactions to 360° feedback. *Bulletin of Psychological Type* 19: 14-18.

Thompson, H. L. 1998a. Type languages, dialects, styles and the extraverted function: Is there a relationship? Unpublished paper, High Performing Systems, Inc.

Thompson, H. L. 1998b. Using the Communication Wheel. *Bulletin of Psychological Type* 21: 10-14.

Thompson, H. L. 1999. Multiple-modality feedback systems for type. *Bulletin of Psychological Type* 22: 14-18.

Thorne, A. 1987. The press of personality: A study of conversations between introverts and extraverts. *Journal of Personality and Social Psychology* 53: 718-26.

Thorne, A. and H. Gough. 1991. *Portraits of Type*. Palo Alto CA: Consulting Psychologists Press.

Tieger, P. D. and B. Barron-Tieger. 1997. *Nature by Nurture.* London: Little, Brown and Co.

Tieger, P. D. and B. Barron-Tieger. 1998. *The Art of SpeedReading People.* London: Little, Brown and Co.

Tieger, P. D. and B. Barron-Tieger. 2000. *Just Your Type.* London: Little, Brown and Co.

Tracey, T. J. G. 2000. Issues in the analysis and interpretation of quantitative data: deinstitutionalization of the null hypothesis test. In S. D. Brown, and R. W. Lent, eds., *Handbook of Counselling Psychology.* 3rd ed. Chichester: Wiley.

Vollrath, M. and S. Torgersen. 2002. Who takes health risks? A probe into eight personality types. *Personality and Individual Differences* 32: 1185-97.

Walck, C. L. 1992. The relationship between Indicator type and "true type": Slight preferences and the verification process. *Journal of Psychological Type* 23: 17-21.

Ware, R. and M. Rytting. 1989. Identification of J-P preference by viewing interiors of automobiles. *Journal of Psychological Type* 18: 63-65.

Ware, R. and C. Yokomoto. 1985. Perceived accuracy of Myers-Briggs Type Indicator descriptions using Keirsey profiles. *Journal of Psychological Type* 10: 27-31.

Watson, D. and L. A. Clark. 1997. Extraversion and its positive emotional core. In R. Hogan, J. Johnson, and S. Briggs, eds., *Handbook of Personality Psychology,* 767-93. San Diego CA: Academic Press.

Watson, D. and A. Tellegen. 1985. Toward a consensual structure of mood. *Psychological Bulletin* 98: 219-35.

Wessley, S. 2001. Randomised controlled trials: The gold standard. In C. Mace, S. Moorey, and B. Roberts, eds., *Evidence in the Psychological Therapies.* Hove: Brunner-Routledge.

White, J. D. 1999. Personality, temperament and ADHD: A review of the literature. *Personality and Individual Differences* 27: 589-98.

Winter, D. G., O. P. John, A. J. Stewart, E. C. Klohnen, and L. E. Duncan. 1998. Traits and motives: Toward an integration of two traditions in personality research. *Psychological Review* 105: 230-50.

Woolhouse, L. S. 1996. An Experimental Study of Individual Differences in Intuition: Preference and Process. Ph.D. diss., University of East London.

Woolhouse, L. S. and R. Bayne. 2000. Personality and the use of intuition: Individual differences in strategy and performance on an implicit learning task. *European Journal of Personality* 14: 157-69.

York, K. L. and O. P. John. 1992. The four faces of Eve: A typological analysis of women's personality at midlife. *Journal of Personality and Social Psychology* 63: 494-508.

INDEX

Murphy, E. 39, 141

Murray, W. D. G. 31, 90, 131

Myers, I. B. 22, 25, 30, 32, 35, 36, 46, 51, 53-57, 75, 83, 93, 99, 143

Myers, K. D. 12, 23, 35, 38, 40, 93

Myers, P. 35, 39, 54-57, 99

Myers, S. 74, 77, 91, 93

N

Nardi, D. 26, 31, 75, 92, 96, 139

Niednagel, J. P. 119, 120, 145, 146

Neuroticism. *See* Anxiety

nonverbal communication 106, 131, 137-139

O

observing type accurately. *See* accuracy

Openness to experience 10, 11, 22, 52, 53

P

Pearman, R. R. 36, 37, 93

Pennebaker, J. W. 131

Perceiving 22, 23, 56-59, 90, 91, 99, 131, 142
    and flexibility 23, 145

personality theory 12, 25-27, 127, 140
    McAdams's framework 25-27

Plomin, R. 15-18

Pratt, C. D. 52, 53, 55, 99

Provost, J. A. 98, 133, 142

preference 12-27, 31, 33, 34, 38, 41, 45-49, 54, 63, 64, 76, 80, 83, 93
    and "appetite" 17
    and "basic" tendencies 15, 18, 19, 32, 46, 83
    and constructivism 19, 20
    and genetic influences 14-20, 27

Q

Quenk, N. L. 14, 34, 35, 39, 46, 80

R

realist (approach to personality) 19, 20

real self 14, 15, 19

report form 91

research styles 4, 5

research techniques 4, 5